Pope John Paul II

Lord Longford

Pope John Paul II

An Authorized Biography

MICHAEL JOSEPH/RAINBIRD

First published in Great Britain in 1982 by Michael Joseph Ltd,
44 Bedford Square, London WC1B 3DU and
George Rainbird Ltd, 40 Park Street, London W1Y 4DE

This book was designed and produced by George Rainbird Ltd
House Editor: Elizabeth Blair
Designer: Martin Bristow
Picture Researcher: Tom Graves
Indexer: Vicki Robinson

ISBN 0 7181 2127 9

Nihil obstat Father Anton Cowan (Censor)
Imprimatur Monsignor David Norris V.G.
Westminster, 8 December 1981

The *Nihil obstat* and *Imprimatur* are a declaration that a book or
pamphlet is considered to be free from doctrinal or moral error.
It is not implied that those who have granted the *Nihil obstat* and
Imprimatur agree with the content, opinions or statements expressed.

Text set by Oliver Burridge and Company Limited, Crawley, England
Colour origination by Gilchrist Brothers Limited, Leeds, England
Printed and bound in Italy by Arnoldo Mondadori Editore, Verona

Illustration Acknowledgments: Bord Failte (Irish Tourist Board), 116; British Museum, 212; Felici, Rome, 1, 2, 14, 16, 20, 23, 26, 27, 28, 30, 48, 50, 56, 67, 78, 79, 80, 82, 87, 88, 89, 90, 91, 94, 98, 99, 105, 108, 112, 115, 117, 118, 125, 126, 127, 128, 129, 130, 131, 134, 137, 138, 139, 140, 141, 145, 146, 149, 151, 152, 155, 158 (*below*), 159, 161, 162, 165, 166 (*above*), 167, 171, 172, 173 (*above*), 176, 180, 183, 187, 191, 192, 193, 194, 195, 196, 198, 199, 202, 205; Tim Graham, 119, 120, 121, 123, 157, 158 (*above*); Bill Gribbin, 221; Robert Harding Picture Library, 32, 63, 86, 107, 109, 181, 190; Interpress, Warsaw, 44, 46, 59, 60, 64, 68, 69, 71, 72, 77, 85; *L'Osservatore Romano*, 184; John MacClancy, 43; Mansell Collection, 211, 213; Arnoldo Mondadori Editore, 147; National Portrait Gallery, London, 209, 210, 217, 219; Rainbird, 54, 190, 213; Rex Features/Sipa, 11, 19, 37, 47, 73, 74, 92, 97, 103, 114, 143, 146, 147, 170 (*above*), 173 (*below*), 177, 178, 179, 182, 200, 201, 203; Scala, 12–13, 55, 188–9; Frank Spooner/Gamma, 8, 10, 24, 25, 33, 34, 35, 36, 38, 39, 40, 53, 100, 102, 106, 110, 111, 113, 122, 124, 133, 166 (*below*), 169, 170 (*below*), 175; ZEFA, 41, 143

Author's Acknowledgments: It is impossible for me to thank all those who have helped me either in conversation or by their writing to compile this book. First of all I must express my deep indebtedness to His Holiness the Pope for granting me a private audience. In Rome, Archbishop Deskur and Bishop Agnellus Andrew took immense trouble in different ways. In England, my special gratitude goes to Cardinal Hume, Archbishop Worlock, Bishop Murphy O'Connor, and Monsignor Brown, and to the staff of *The Universe* office.
   A number of English Catholics have been kind enough to record their feelings about the coming visit. The Duke of Norfolk and my wife have been quoted at length. I have consulted many books in my research and all have been helpful. I must pay particular tribute to Mary Craig's *Man From a Far Country*; the work of Peter Hebblethwaite, where it is unnecessary to agree with everything he writes to recognize the incisiveness of his style; and Peter Nichols. I thank Hutchinson & Co. for permission to quote from *The Easter Vigil and Other Poems* by Karol Wojtyla.

Contents

Foreword by Cardinal Hume

The election of a Polish Cardinal as Pope in the autumn of 1978 aroused the curiosity and interest of the whole world. Almost overnight we were confronted with a range of books, often written at great speed, which tried to answer the inevitable questions that people were asking about the life of the man himself, his background, his qualities, and the significance of his election, the first non-Italian Pope in four hundred years and the first ever Slav Pope. Since 1978, the almost ceaseless journeys of the Holy Father have been followed closely by the media. Even more books have been published recording his activity. It seems difficult to satisfy the appetite of the general public, to say nothing of those who are committed Christians.

Now Pope John Paul II is to visit Britain, the first successor of St Peter to set foot on these shores. As the visit draws nearer a particular interest is growing. Given the turbulent religious history of this country, given the longstanding bitterness which separated these islands from the visible unity of the Roman Catholic Church, it is hardly surprising that many see the coming of the Pope as an event of major historical, religious and ecumenical significance. Certainly there are many people in all the Christian Churches here who pray that it may further the cause of Christian unity. In these circumstances, a great many people want to read about the personality and attitudes of this great man. They want a chance to assess the three years of his ministry as Pope, to see whether what he has done matches the expectations of the world at the time of his election.

Readers of this book will come to it with different needs and from differing viewpoints. Roman Catholics are naturally always interested in their supreme pastor. Yet, even among them, there is no doubt that the present Pope has achieved something of a breakthrough in communication. I doubt if there would be any Catholics today who did not have at least some knowledge of our present Pope and of where he stands on most of the major religious and moral issues. He has an unrivalled rapport with mass audiences. He communicates well on television. His encyclical letters are certainly lengthy, but they speak with rare passion and directness. Catholics look to him then with confidence for words of faith and for guidance. In the context of his visit to Britain, they will be eager to retrace his early days, his life as Church leader and his subsequent ministry as Pope.

Non-Catholic Christians too, have responded to him with unusual respect and warmth. They disagree on some matters, but most seem to find his fearless affirmation of the Gospel a source of hope and encouragement. In a particular way, they scrutinize his message and his actions to see what his particular ministry signifies for the cause of Christian unity. As he prepares to come to Britain, there are many who want to put the recent past into some sort of order and perspective. They want to prepare realistically and spiritually for whatever Christian challenge he may bring.

Even those who normally have little conscious link with the institutional Christian Church have sensed the special quality of Pope John Paul. Intrigued by his background, they have watched with sympathy his bold leadership of those who live under the Communist regimes of Eastern Europe. They applaud his support for human rights, his evident sympathy for the poor and dispossessed. They have warmed to his humanity. They too, as the visit approaches will want to have in their hands a portrait of this man who is so deeply spiritual and so obviously human.

In many ways he identifies with the struggle and pain of so many people. He suffered the early loss of parents and family. He knew the harshness of physical labour. He is used to deprivation. He has endured opposition and restriction of personal liberty under dictatorships. He has suffered the violence of a terrorist attack. He can be seen as a symbolic figure of this troubled age.

Lord Longford's book then, meets a widely-felt need. He has drawn on published sources and talked to many who have lived and worked alongside the Holy Father. He brings together in a comprehensive way the earlier life of Karol Wojtyla and his present ministry as Pope John Paul II. He has tried not to interpose himself between the Pope and the reader. In general his approval is balanced and objective. We owe Lord Longford a debt of gratitude for his skill in presenting in a brief yet careful way a remarkable period in the recent history of the Catholic Church.

I sincerely hope that this life of Pope John Paul II will help to prepare people generally for his historic visit. Although he comes primarily to be with the Roman Catholic community, I am convinced he will be welcomed at every level of our national life. Lord Longford has contributed to that welcome.

CARDINAL BASIL HUME
December, 1981   Archbishop of Westminster

Chapter 1

'We have a Pope'

T HE TENSION MOUNTED. The hundred thousand people waiting in St Peter's Square were excited and restless. By the
evening of 16 October 1978, the Cardinals had been in conclave in the Sistine Chapel for more than two days. Not a long time
by ordinary standards, but a day longer than when, a little more than
a month earlier, Pope John Paul I had been elected. His tragic death,
after he had become so greatly loved in so short a time, added an
undercurrent of anxiety. Then at 6.18 p.m. the white smoke rose
from the chimney of the Sistine Chapel, strong and clear and unmistakeable. There was a burst of excited applause; everyone pressed
forward towards the central balcony of St Peter's Basilica, from
where the announcement of the new Pope would be made. Half an
hour later the window above the balcony opened slowly. Cardinal
Pericle Felici stepped forward. 'I announce to you a great joy,' he
proclaimed in the time-honoured words, '*Habemus Papam*' (We have
a Pope). The crowd roared with pleasure, then waited in eager
silence. The name Karolum Wojtyla meant little or nothing to the
crowd as a whole. They seemed a little bewildered.

Cardinal Felici proceeded: '*qui sibi nomen imposuit Joannes Paulus
Secundus*' (who has taken the name of John Paul II). That produced
some cheering; the identity of the new Pope was beginning to sink
in; the fact that he was a non-Italian and a Pole. There were cries of
'*Ecco. E il Polacco*'. The enthusiasm grew but it was still guarded. Then
at 7.22 p.m. the new Pope appeared on the balcony. It was Cardinal
Wojtyla of Cracow, aged fifty-eight, the first Pope to come from
Eastern Europe, and from a nation under Communist rule. The
youngest Pope for more than a century, he was a powerfully built
man, with the strongest kind of Slavonic face, and a smile totally
different from that of his predecessor but no less winning. His
audience was expecting the traditional Latin blessing *Urbi et Orbi* (to
the Church and the world). But instead he addressed them first in resounding tones in a barely accented Italian: '*Carissimi fratelli e sorelle*
– dearly beloved brothers and sisters, we are all still saddened by the
death of our beloved Pope John Paul I and so the Cardinals have

OPPOSITE The new Pope,
John Paul II, appears for the
first time on the balcony of
St Peter's Basilica.

9

The Sistine Chapel where the Cardinals of the Sacred College meet to elect a new Pope.

called for a new Bishop of Rome. They have called him from a far-away country, faraway and yet close, because of our communion in the traditions of the Church. I was afraid to accept that responsibility, yet I do so in a spirit of obedience to the Lord and total faithfulness to Mary, our most holy Mother.'

The crowd were already with him, but he went on to win them over completely: 'I do not know if I can express myself in your – no – our Italian tongue. If I make mistakes you will have to correct me.' This deliberate gesture from a magnificent linguist swept them away. The applause that followed the blessing was prolonged and tumultuous.

It is easy with hindsight to say that the time had clearly come for the election of a non-Italian Pope and that Cardinal Wojtyla was the obvious candidate. But, at the time, he had appeared on practically nobody's list of likely candidates.

Cardinal Wojtyla was admittedly little known in Britain. But those who did know him, or knew Poland well, greeted the election with immense enthusiasm. Archbishop Worlock of Liverpool had sat with the Pope for thirteen years on the Council of the Laity. He made no secret of his joy about the news. He described Wojtyla as having 'the greatest intellect I have ever met', and continued, 'he is a man of wonderfully exuberant good spirits. He has a great love for his country. His powers of mental analysis and courage under all circumstances are equally remarkable.'

In Poland, the Pastor of Cracow's Wawel Cathedral learned of the election of Cardinal Wojtyla as Pope on the 7 p.m. news on the radio. 'The old man's hands were shaking with excitement when he received telephone calls from all over the city,' writes Tadeusz Karolak in *John Paul II.* Joyful and enthusiastic crowds of people flooded into the market place. Nuns were seen dancing in the streets. At midnight, the Cathedral echoed with joyful hymns and the service of thanksgiving was celebrated. In Wadowice, Pope John Paul's home parish, the Dean, Fr Edward Zacher, broke down in tears and shouted with joy. Zacher, Karol Wojtyla's old teacher, opened the thick, well-worn register of Births and on page 549, under the name Karol Wojtyla wrote: *ad summum pontificatum electus et imposuit sibi nomen Johannes Paulus secundus* (elected to the highest office of the Church and chose for himself the name of John Paul II). When Fr Zacher had given his fifth sermon, in honour of his former pupil, he told the Cardinal, as Wojtyla then was, that there was only one more sermon like that left to him to deliver: when the Cardinal became Pope. The Cardinal had commented that there would never be a sixth sermon. 'And he didn't keep his word for the first time in his life,' said the old priest laughingly and lovingly.

OVERLEAF Christ gives the keys of the Church of the Church to St Peter. A painting in the Sistine Chapel of the Vatican by Perugino.

The new Pope acknowledges the cheers of the crowd in St Peter's Square after his election.

The Catholic Church has its roots in the words used by Christ to Simon: 'Thou art Peter, and upon this rock I will build this Church.' So Peter became the first Pope and the founder of the Roman Church. He is buried at the foot of the Vatican hill.

Among Peter's successors there have been great saints, great statesmen and great patrons of the arts. There have been a few whose morals cannot easily be condoned. Their characters, their achievements, their claims, spiritual and temporal, have figured largely in the history of the last two thousand years and produced their share of controversy.

The modern history of the Church begins when Pope John XXIII (1958-63) summoned the Second Vatican Council in January 1959. There had been no Council for over a century and John XXIII felt the time had come for the Church to put its own house in order. John XXIII was dead within a year but he had altered the Church irreversibly. Throughout the world, Catholics and non-Catholics had responded unrestrainedly to him. One of the few really bigoted anti-Catholics among men I have met of genuine distinction went so far as to tell me, 'I can't help liking that old man of yours'.

Pope John XXIII opened the windows of the Church to the entire world, not least the Communist countries. In the encyclical *Pacem in Terris*, he distinguished sharply between atheism and atheists in a way that disturbed his conservative advisers. In 1963 he was awarded the Balzam Peace Prize, a truly international reward; the Soviet leader, Khrushchev, like John of peasant stock, cast a vote in his favour. Then on 3 June 1958 he died. What, at the age of eighty-two, would he have gone on to accomplish? The achievement of those four years will stand for all time.

Before he became Pope John XXIII, Cardinal Roncalli was little known in the world at large, and unknown in England except to a few specialists. When it was announced that Roncalli, an old man of seventy-eight, had been elected there was widespread disappointment. It was assumed not unreasonably that he had been chosen as a stop-gap, and that action of any significant kind would be postponed for the next few years.

Angelo Roncalli came of a family of peasant farmers from the little village of Sotto il Monte in the strongly Catholic province of Bergamo in Lombardy. He had served as a sergeant in the Italian Army in World War I and more recently in the Papal Diplomatic Service in Bulgaria, Turkey and Paris. At the time of his election, he was the patriarch of Venice. Anyone who has read his diary *Journey of a Soul* would realize that here was a man of quite extraordinary spiritual purpose. But at the time John XXIII became Pope, there can have been few who knew anything about this aspect of him.

OPPOSITE Pope John Paul II praying at the tomb of St Peter in the crypt of St Peter's Basilica.

15

OPPOSITE Pope John XXIII

The idea that John XXIII would be a stop-gap was soon proved wonderfully wrong. Almost at once the world began to hear tales of his kindness and congeniality. There are numerous stories about the ways in which he changed the face of the Papacy: he stood his gardener a glass of wine; he visited the inmates of a prison; he insisted on breaking the custom that had grown up by which a Pope always eats alone, and invited his peasant brothers to his table and on occasions insisted on a friend sharing his lunch; he resumed the *de tabella* conferences with the Cardinals which the more austere and less approachable Pius XII had discontinued. Few would dispute, as Christopher Hollis has said, that 'he won the affection of men and women throughout the world, inside and outside his own communion, to an extent for which history has few parallels.'

John XXIII's universal popularity gave him an opportunity, unique up to that time, to speak to the world. The great social encyclicals *Rerem Novarum* (1891) and *Quadragesimo Anno* (1931) stated the Church's teachings on the problems of social justice. But these did not have much to say which was relevant in the 1960s to the tremendous issues of international social tension, as distinct from those of justice within a nation. Pope John was a real pioneer in this, as in other respects. Taking a world rather than a national view of social conditions in different countries, he wrote in his encyclical, *Mater et Magistra*: 'It is therefore obvious that the solidarity of the human race and Christian brotherhood demand the elimination as far as possible of these discrepancies. With this object in view people all over the world must co-operate actively with one another in all sorts of ways so as to facilitate the movement of goods, capital and men from one country to another.'

He went on to insist 'that the solidarity that binds all men together as members of a common family make it impossible for wealthy nations to look with indifference upon the hunger, misery and poverty of other nations, whose citizens were unable to enjoy even elementary human rights. The nations of the world are becoming more and more dependent on one another but, even so, it will not be possible to preserve a lasting peace so long as these glaring economic and social inequalities persist.' Here was a drastic warning that implied a need for revolutionary international action which would have astonished Pius XI, who had reigned only thirty years earlier.

Mater et Magistra was more novel in spirit than his equally great encyclical on peace, *Pacem in Terris*, in which he pleaded for negotiation and conciliation. Other Popes had begged the nations of the world to renounce the horrors of war and warlike poverties. There had never been a Pope, however, who was so conscious that the world was indeed one family, and that any action by one nation of a warlike character made a world war that much more probable.

The whole necessity of the reform of the Church itself became at once his inspiration and obsession. He summoned the Second Vatican Council of the Bishops of the world to advise him. The Second Vatican Council was opened by Pope John in St Peter's on 2 October 1962. Exactly 2,540 Bishops had come from every corner of the earth, little more than a third of them from European sees. The session began at 8.30 in the morning. Soon afterwards Pope John was carried in amid tremendous cheers. He took his seat, mitre and tiara in hand. Mass was sung and then he received the homage of the Cardinals. He delivered a discourse remarkably devoid of platitudes, but not dogmatic; he was waiting for the advice of the Bishops. He said that this was an age in which the Church should maintain her authority, 'with the medicine of mercy, rather than severity'. He spoke with notable sympathy for those who were not of the Catholic world. He commended the deliberations of the Bishops to the Holy Spirit.

He said that the task of the Council was not to define new documents. It was an opportunity for the Church 'to bring herself up to date where required'. He asserted that the doctrines of the Church were immutable but that the method of imparting them must change from generation to generation, admitting that this was a formulation which Catholics would find easier than non-Catholics to accept unreservedly. But he maintained that many non-Catholics would agree that for nearly 2,000 years the Holy Spirit has been at work through the Catholic and maybe other churches, even though its voice has never been perfectly interpreted.

What was the Pope's purpose? It has been defined and re-defined many times. Fr Francis Murphy, a recognized if controversial expert on the Papacy, has put it as concisely as anyone. 'What John actually desired was a reformation of the Church, in the sense of bringing it back to its essential function as the presence of Jesus Christ in the world.' But John XXIII was as clear about the kind of means that were necessary as about the end. He well knew that, however long he was spared, he could not carry through the revolution he contemplated by dictatorial methods. The whole Church must be involved in the far-reaching changes. There must be an altogether new formula for discussion; hence the summoning of the Council, from which could be expected the first steps towards an endless process of renewal. It was well known from the beginning that a number of Cardinals of high standing were suspicious of and opposed to the whole enterprise. The very idea of a 'free for all' on matters that went to the heart of the Church's existence filled them with agitation

OPPOSITE Pope Paul VI

18

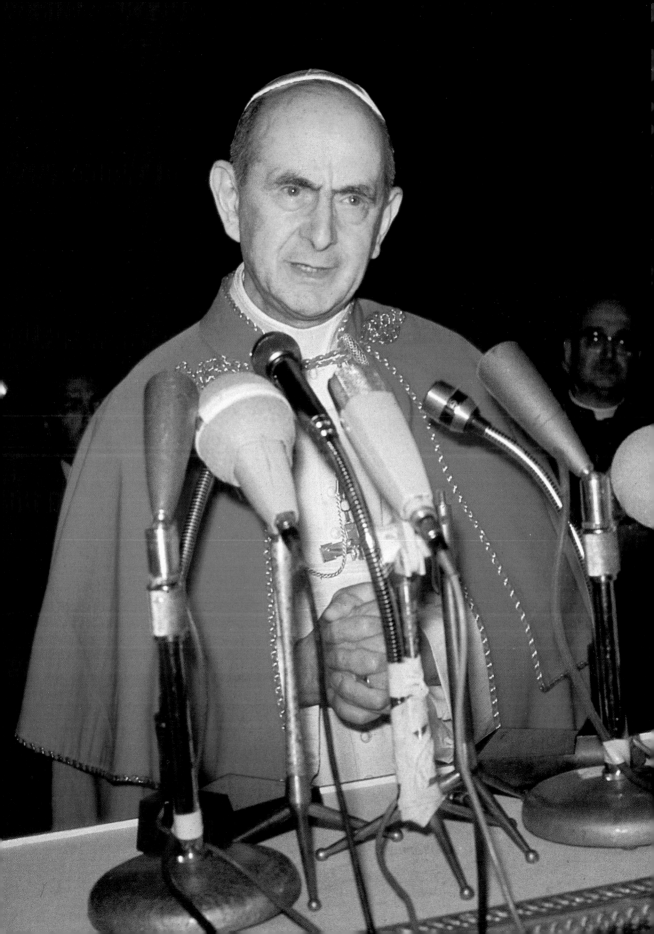

and alarm. If they were alive today it might be that they would say 'I told you so' in suitable ecclesiastical language. Everyone must agree that the Catholic Church in the last twenty years has been 'turned upside down'. For the better? The vast majority of Catholics think so. And so, without qualification, do I.

John XXIII's successor, Cardinal Montini, who took the name Paul VI (1963–78), was a man of fine intellectual talents and sensitive soul. He had been born of a bourgeois family in northern Italy in 1898. His father was a banker and an agricultural entrepreneur who controlled the local newspaper and championed Catholic causes. His mother was, in Fr Francis Murphy's words, 'a delicate but determined activist, involved in social and charitable enterprises'.

Karol, Cardinal Wojtyla standing beside Pope Paul VI.

He was exempted from War Service on physical grounds and spent much of World War I in charitable activities and studying theology at home. When he was ordained priest in 1920 he had had a thoroughly religious upbringing. He was a man of wide culture and had an intense interest in international affairs. In the post-war period, he presided with Monsignor Tardini over the Holy See's internal and external dealings. In 1954 he was relieved of his position as personal adviser to Pope Pius XII and was consecrated Archbishop of Milan. It seemed that he had been 'kicked upstairs'. It remained to Pope John XXIII to make him a Cardinal in 1958.

It is easy and not altogether audacious to contrast the inward-looking Paul VI – Pope John is supposed to have called him 'Hamlet' – with John's outgoing temperament. In fact, Montini, a younger man, took much more positive steps than John XXIII to break out of the Vatican and be seen by the world. John had embarked on walking tours in Rome, visited hospitals and gaols, orphanages and dying friends and travelled by train to Loretto in the Abruzzi mountains. Paul, however, travelled wide and far. Among the countries he visited were the Holy Land, India, Turkey, America, the Philippines, Australia, Samoa, Indonesia, Hong Kong and Singapore. He always had a particular concern to visit poverty-stricken areas of the world.

It was no fault of Pope Paul's that he did not succeed in visiting Poland. He did all he could to go to Warsaw in 1966 for the one-thousandth anniversary of the founding of the Polish nation. But the Communist regime, whose relationship with the Primate, Cardinal Wyszynski and the Church in Poland generally was very strained at that time, prevented the visit.

In his general dealings with Communist countries Paul VI followed in the steps of Pope John in distinguishing between the sin and the sinner, atheism and atheists. He himself inaugurated a political policy that carried John's so-called 'opening to the left' a long way forward. He welcomed statesmen and the heads of nations of every persuasion to the Vatican. His visitors included Communist leaders such as Podgorny, Gromyko, Tito, Gierek, Ceausescu, revolutionary Socialists from Asia and Africa, and representatives of the capitalist West. To quote Fr Murphy again: 'In his vision of the Church's obligation, he preached the Gospel to every nation, including continental China.'

On the international front, his main attitudes were outspokenly progressive. His encyclical on the development of peoples and his apostolic call to action were radical documents. In the United Nations' General Assembly in New York in October 1965, he carried much conviction with his cry, 'No more war. War never again.' He

condemned injustice, governmental violence and economic exploitation in no uncertain terms, pointing out that 'violence is not in
keeping with the Gospel'.

Internally, Pope Paul showed a considerable reforming zeal,
though he did not go as far as reformers wished. He reduced the
number of Italian heads of Curial Congregations, the equivalent of
cabinet ministers, to four. He appointed a Frenchman as Secretary
of State and a Yugoslav, a Brazilian, an American, and a Canadian
to other top positions.

Following the recommendations of the Council, he instituted a
Roman Synod of Bishops. In 1967 and 1969, 1971, 1974 and 1977
Cardinals and Bishops from all round the world were brought to
Rome for discussions. He instituted a Synodal Secretariat in Rome
to give continuity and reality to the deliberations of the Bishops. In
his creation of Cardinals, he ranged far and wide to give the Church
an international image.

Paul VI 'reigned' for fifteen years. He will be remembered by many
too readily, and quite unfairly, for his encyclical *Humanae Vitae* and
its firm confirmation of the Church's ban on artificial birth control
after a commission of Bishops, set up by himself, had recommended
that the ban be abolished. He was equally firm in re-asserting the
celibacy of the priesthood. As a result he is often thought a conservative Pope. His energy and initiative inevitably weakened as he
approached his eightieth year. But it is not fair to judge him solely
on this last stage of his life. By taking the title of Paul, he had
declared for innovation and he was himself an innovator to the end,
giving effect to the vision that had inspired Pope John XXIII to call
the Council. In addition, Paul VI stood for clerical reform, bringing
the liturgy closer to the people; for the collegiate principle, though
in regard to birth control he set it aside; and for ecumenical progress.
He also held out the hand of friendship in no uncertain terms towards
the Anglican Church.

But despite this creditable record, at the time of his death Paul VI
was still a rather shadowy figure in some countries, including
Britain. Even those at the centre of things who knew him best and
admired him the most felt that someone completely different was
needed next time.

Fr Greely, the journalist and author, summed up the prevailing
undercurrent of feeling when he wrote: 'The Catholic Church
needs a holy man with a smile.' With the Holy Spirit even more in
evidence than usual, that is precisely what the Catholic Church got;
but for little more than a month.

The voting in the conclave is secret but it appears that the Curia,
the vast Vatican Civil Service, or at any rate its leaders, were deter-

The funeral of Pope Paul VI
in St Peter's Square, August
1978

mined to defeat two of the supposedly strongest candidates. Their
support initially went to the elderly Cardinal Siri, a self-confessed
conservative of vast experience. It seems that, on the first ballot,
Cardinal Siri obtained thirty-five votes and Cardinal Luciani twenty-
three. When the Curia realized that a majority for Cardinal Siri
could not be put together, it is said that they switched their allegiance
to Cardinal Luciani. As a non-curial Italian Pope of recognized
personal goodness, he would presumably be fairly amenable to
official advice. Luciani swept ahead on the third ballot. He had over
ninety votes and his nearest rival no more than seventeen. His triumph was therefore overwhelming. But once he was elected in 1978,
Pope John Paul I, as he designated himself, 'the Holy man with a
smile', took everyone by surprise. He was going to be a new kind of
Pope in a number of ways including the simplicity of his lifestyle.
His famous smile carried him readily into the affections of the waiting
world.

Cardinal Hume referred to the new Pope as 'God's candidate',
echoing the thoughts of many. John Paul I showed himself possessed,
on the surface at least, of a kind of divine self-confidence, although
how great a strain he felt the role of Pope imposed upon him no one
can know. Soon after his election he received the Cardinals as a body.
He tossed aside as 'too unctuous' the speech prepared for him. He
told the Cardinals that he expected their full co-operation. This, he

said, would require at times a sacrifice and a change of viewpoint on their part. He, not they, would govern and determine Church policy and its implementation. This was plain-speaking with a vengeance. He had announced that his installation as Pope would be a simple Mass, before which he would be invested with a pallium, a white woollen stole decorated with six black Latin crosses. Out went the Coronation ceremony with the tiara, the throne and all the other manifestations of worldly glory. John Paul I was taking the Papacy back to Christ, who had said: 'My kingdom is not of this world.'

No one will ever know whether John Paul I could have carried the burden of the Papacy and survived. The matter would never be put to the test. On Friday, 29 October 1978, only thirty-three days after his election, the world learned that he had passed away, working, or over-working, to the last.

Meanwhile, what of Karol Wojtyla? Pope Paul VI had died on 6 October 1978. Cardinal Wojtyla went to the Franciscan monastery of Kalwaria to say Mass for him. This monastery, which was near to his birthplace of Wadowice, was very dear to Wojtyla. He often took groups of pilgrims there to make the Way of the Cross with him. On this occasion he remained a long time in prayer. The monks could see that he was strained and worried. Then he set off for Rome and when he returned he looked quite different. He was altogether his normal cheerful self. One must conclude that the possibility of being elected Pope had cast a shadow over him before he went to Rome. His relief when John Paul I was elected was unmistakeable.

OPPOSITE Pope John Paul I

Pope John Paul I, 'The Holy man with a smile'

The body of Pope John
Paul I lying in state in St
Peter's.

He offered fervent prayers for the new Pope and called all members
of his diocese to join with him.

During the short Papacy of Pope John Paul I, Cardinal Wojtyla
signed one final document which he had done much to inspire. It
was a strong appeal to the Polish government to allow the Church
access to the media. The Church's only mouthpiece was the Catholic
press, itself heavily censored. The embargo on the broadcasting of
religious services in Poland would only be broken when his own
inauguration as Pope was broadcast live from Rome, and even then
it was shown only on local television programmes.

When Pope John Paul I died, Cardinal Wojytla went to Kalwaria
once more. He said Mass before the altar dedicated to Maximilian
Kolbe, the priest who had shown such courage and self-sacrifice in
Auschwitz during World War II. He prayed with all his heart that
the Cardinals would make a wise choice. His last words before he
left for Rome have become historic: 'My friends, pray for me.' I was
present at the Coronation of Queen Elizabeth II in Westminster
Abbey and will never forget the depth of feeling she evoked when
she called on the great congregation and the millions outside to give
her their prayers. It is legitimate to bring together those two acts of
total commitment.

It was recognized that the second conclave would be a strenuous
affair. In the event, it seems that the conclusion was reached after

eight ballots. It is still not quite clear whether Pope John Paul I had been elected after three or four ballots. The decision to choose a non-Italian was sensational. The decision to choose a Pope from behind the Iron Curtain, and this very remarkable man in particular, was not surprising once the great break with tradition had been made.

There is a lot of evidence to indicate that Cardinal Wojtyla was not the front runner in the minds of most of the Cardinals at the beginning of the conclave. It seems certain that a non-Italian was considered only after the Italian candidates had been tried and had failed to gain the seventy-five votes needed. There was strong support for Cardinal Siri once more, and for Cardinal Benelli whose experience of high Vatican policy was unique and who had recently had pastoral experience in Florence. But the vital fact is that the Italian 'candidates' cancelled each other out. At last the way was open for the best available non-Italian. We are told that the name of Cardinal Wojtyla was mentioned every now and then while the idea of an Italian Pope was still prevalent. When the Italians failed to produce a Pope on the sixth ballot, support switched to Wojtyla. He went right ahead on the seventh ballot and was elected with over ninety votes on the eighth ballot.

Little thought, it seems, was given to the political implications of the election of a man from behind the Iron Curtain. Looking back now, it seems that, once the tradition of an Italian Pope had been

The new Pope, John Paul II, with some of his Cardinals after his election

broken, Wojtyla had everything to recommend him: his background and intellectual gifts, not to mention the personal benevolence already so well known in Poland. The collapse under strain of Pope John Paul I must be said to have influenced many in favour of a younger man of such exceptional physical and mental vigour. On this occasion, once again it did not need any special exertion on the part of the Holy Spirit to designate the right man for the office.

The Polish President and his Minister for Religion were present at the Installation Mass of John Paul II. Like his predecessor, John Paul II chose to be invested with a pallium, rather than crowned with a papal tiara. At his first formal meetings with the Cardinals, he stressed his commitment to collegiality and ecumenism and emphasized the need for new structures to make collegiality work. For the key position of Secretary of State he chose a professional diplomat, Cardinal Casseroli, who would ensure that diplomatic objectives served the pastoral ends of the Church and who was skilled in dealing with Communist regimes. He himself had all the pastoral experience required for leadership.

OPPOSITE Pope John Paul II greets the crowds in St Peter's Square after the Mass following his election.

Chapter 2

The Making of a Priest
1920-1946

K AROL W OJTYLA was born in the market town of Wadowice fifty kilometres southwest of Cracow on 18 May 1920. The first nineteen years of his life were passed during the only period of independence that Poland, once a mighty nation, has known since the ruthless partitions of the eighteenth century.

For over one thousand years the Church has been the true custodian of Poland's national tradition and identity. There is surely no village in Poland where the priest is not very much the dominant personality of his parish, despite the fact that for the last forty years the actual rulers have been Russian and German invaders or, since World War II, Polish Communists owing their power entirely to the military might of Russia.

To quote George Blazynski in his vivid book *John Paul II: A Man from Kracow*, 'There are four landmarks of human hope and tragedy under whose shadows Wojtyla grew up and worked, and they are all to be found within the single archdiocese of Cracow: the shrine of Czestochowa, the gas chambers of Auschwitz and the city of Cracow, and the blast furnaces of Nowa Huta.'

The shrine of Czestochowa at Jasna Gora is famous both for its monastery in which the painting of the Black Madonna is kept and also as the fortress which held back the Swedish invaders led by Charles X Gustavus in the seventeenth century. Czestochowa is Poland's most revered shrine. On one occasion, over a million pilgrims assembled at Czestochowa to attend Mass and to listen to the sermons of Cardinal Wyszynski, the Primate of Poland, and Cardinal Wojtyla.

Auschwitz is preserved as a memorial to the millions of Jews, Poles, Russians and others gassed by the Nazis in World War II. It too draws its pilgrims, led on occasion by Wojtyla as Archbishop and Cardinal.

Cracow is the capital of the archdiocese. Described by Blazynski as 'at once the Oxford and Winchester of Poland', Cracow is both an historical seat of learning and an ancient capital. We shall be returning also to Nowa Huta, with its huge steelworks, named after

OPPOSITE The Pope on his visit to Poland saying Mass at the shrine of the Black Madonna at Czestochowa.

The sitting-room of the Wojtyla family apartment in Wadowice

Lenin, intended as the Socialist new town in explicit contradiction to the religious devotion of Cracow.

Karol Wojtyla's family circumstances were modest. His birthplace and first home were a rather small apartment at No. 7, Koscielna (Church) Street in Wadowice. His father was a retired army lieutenant, administrative grade, living on a small pension. His family originated from Czaniec, a village to the south. Karol Wojtyla's paternal grandfather was a tailor who married and settled in Wadowice. His mother, Emilia, was a gentle person, whose face in a photograph bears a striking resemblance to the present Pope. Her family came from Silesia, the Austrian-occupied part of Poland. Her children were equipped therefore with German as a second language. She used to push Karol's pram through a neighbour's garden so that he could get some fresh air. The neighbour still remembers Emilia's happy assertion: 'You will see, my Lolek' – this is how he came to be known as a small boy – 'will grow up to be a great man.' She took in sewing to eke out the finances. But she enjoyed poor health, and she died giving birth to her third child, a still-born girl.

OPPOSITE Karol Wojtyla's mother, Emilia, with his brother, Edmund

It has been suggested that the early loss of his mother may have

32

Karol Wojtyla's father, who
was also called Karol

contributed to Wojtyla's passionate attachment to the Virgin Mary in later years, but such a devotion would not be uncommon in Poland. Family hopes had been centred on Lolek's older brother, Edmund, who was fifteen when the younger boy was born. Edmund showed promise of becoming a brilliant doctor but, four years after his mother's death, he also died, as a result of an infection caught in the hospital in which he worked. On his gravestone are inscribed the words: 'Edmund died as a victim of his profession in which he had devoted his young life to suffering humanity.' The patient from whom he had contracted scarlet fever in fact recovered. John Paul II still has a Requiem Mass said every year on the anniversary of Edmund's death at the Franciscan church in Cracow. Father Figlewicz, who taught religion to Karol Wojtyla before being transferred to Cracow, remembers him as a boy in whose behaviour one could perceive the shadow of an early sorrow.

Lolek and his father, the only surviving member of his family, were drawn into the closest of relationships. The father loved Karol dearly, but he was a stern disciplinarian, as his photograph suggests. He cooked for Lolek, washed and ironed his clothes, went for long walks with him, and imparted to him firm religious principles from

Karol Wojtyla with his son, Karol

35

Karol Wojtyla *(second row, second from right)* on a school outing to Wieliczka in 1930. His father *(second row, fourth from right)* is also in the group.

the earliest days. Before going to school each morning, young Lolek stopped off to pray in church.

At the age of seven, he entered the universal or primary school in Wadowice, and at the age of eleven, in 1931, the boys' high school (Gymnasium). Before Karol began his first year of high school, his father had to choose between a state school and two private schools, run by the Pallottine and Carmelite Fathers. There are three probable reasons why he chose a state school: firstly, it had a fine teaching staff and an established reputation; secondly, a state school was not as expensive as a private school; and thirdly, the schools run by the clergy were inclined to guide their pupils towards a theological seminary. Wojtyla's father, though intently religious, wanted his son to make such decisions for himself. In Karol's class there were thirty-two pupils, the sons of farmers in the area, manual workers and the local professional classes. Fr Zacher, who taught him there for six years, gave a striking account of him to Mary Craig, whose description of his early years in her *Man from a Far Country* is enlightening. 'Lolek,' he told her, 'was the nearest thing to a genius I ever had the good fortune to teach.' But he was not only outstandingly good at his books, he was also very popular with his school-

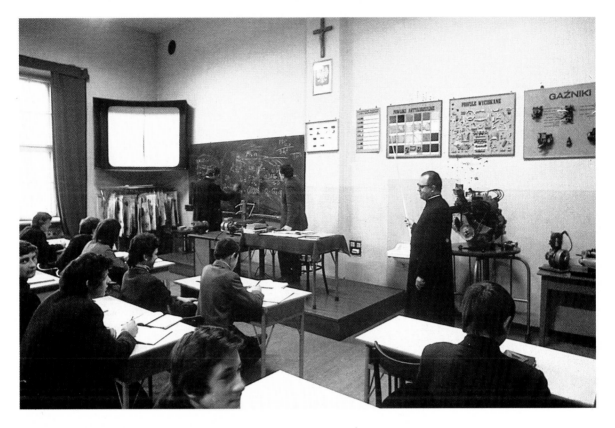

mates. Powerful of build, he was one of the best footballers, usually playing in goal, and loved swimming, canoeing and, most of all, skiing in the nearby Tatras mountains, which exercised from the beginning an abiding fascination for Karol Wojtyla. He loved the poems of Jan Kasprowicz which celebrated the beauty of the Tatras mountains, and he knew and loved the mountain people, the Gorals, whose peculiar patois he understood. All his life, the Tatras have been a refuge, a place for meditation, and stock-taking in times of stress.

It is, however, as an actor that he is best remembered by his school-friends. A visiting director told him: 'One day you will be a great actor.' No one doubted the truth of these words. During Karol Wojtyla's youth, plays were put on in Wadowice by Mieczyslaw Kotlarczyk. He was to have a permanent influence on the future Pope. He would become the founder of the Rhapsodic Theatre in Cracow during the Nazi occupation. Later he was to become famous for his dramatic theory of the living word. In Wadowice, the outline of that theory was already beginning to emerge.

There can be no doubt that this art of the living word expounded over many years by Mieczyslaw Kotlarczyk permeated and inspired

The schoolroom in Wadowice where Karol Wojtyla was once a pupil.

37

Karol Wojtyla as a schoolboy

Karol Wojtyla from youth onwards. It was eventually reflected in the astonishing impact that the future Pope was to make in many different languages on countless millions throughout the world.

Adam Miciewicz was the dominant figure in Polish literature at that time. The national epic poem *Pan Tadeusz: The Last Foray in Lithuania* was written by Miciewicz in exile after the November uprising of 1830 and amid the Great Emigration which followed. It is in twelve cantos, and Karol Wojtyla learned it by heart as a youth. The opening lines would be recited by John Paul II at the close of his inaugural speech after his election as Pope. In the same speech, he

OPPOSITE Karol Wojtyla: his first Communion photograph

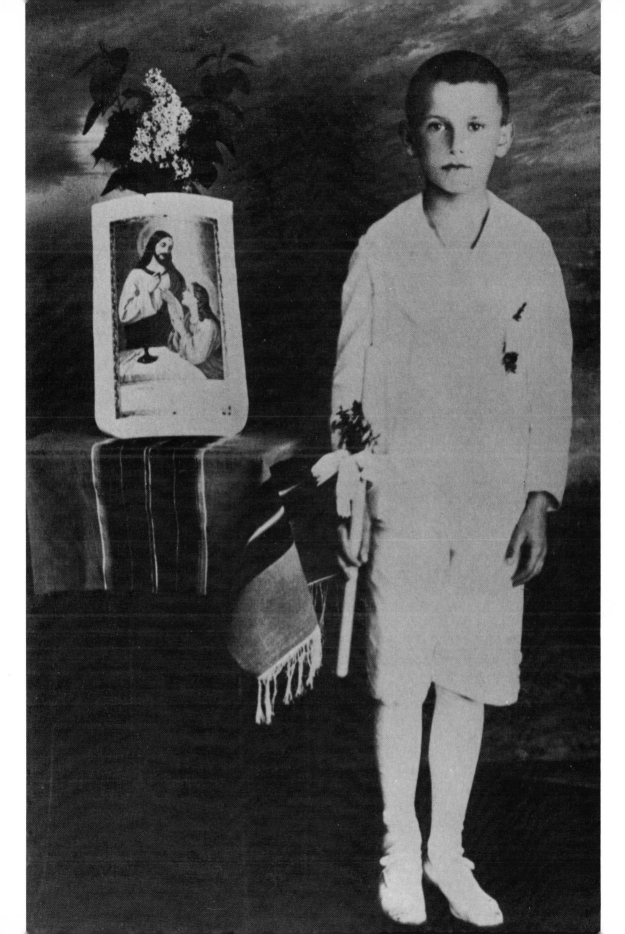

Karol Wojtyla *(back row, far left)* with some classmates

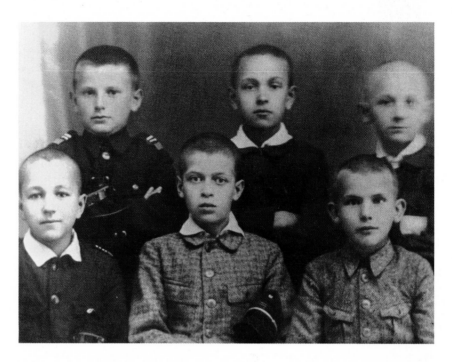

restated his lifelong devotion to the Virgin Mary by quoting the famous lines from *Pan Tadeusz*:

'O Holy Maid, who Czestochowa's shrine
Dost guard and on the Pointed Gateway shine
And watchest Nowogrodek's pinnacle,
As thou didst heal me by a miracle . . .
So by a miracle thou'lt bring us home!'

Karol did not parade his piety though he still stopped each morning to pray in church, and was very active at the school's Marian Society, serving as President for over three years.

When Archbishop, later Cardinal, Sapieha of Cracow visited his school in 1938, Wojtyla was selected to propose the vote of thanks. Then, as always, his voice and bearing were an immediate asset. The Archbishop turned to Fr Zacher and asked: 'Is that boy going to be a priest?' Fr Zacher had, in fact, hoped that Wojtyla would finally choose that vocation, which may have been one reason why he wished to bring him before the eyes of the Archbishop. There are various versions of Zacher's reply. In one he answered: 'It does not look like it at the moment,' but in another he said, 'I do not know. He is in love with the theatre and they have talked him into taking Polish philology.' 'A very great pity,' commented Sapieha. 'He would make a good one.'

In 1938 the Wojtylas, father and son, moved to Cracow. Cracow

OPPOSITE Wawel Cathedral, the seat of the Archbishop of Cracow

is a city which is as beautiful as it is romantic. It is one of the oldest cities in Poland. According to legend, it owes its origins and name to Prince Krak, who slew a dragon and founded a fortified settlement there. It lay on the trade route between Russia, Bohemia and Western Europe, and prospered accordingly. By the middle of the twelfth century it had become the capital of Poland. In 1609 it was supplanted by Warsaw by the Decree of King Sigismund III, but it has always remained the cultural centre of the country. Its university, the Jagiellonian, founded in 1364, is the oldest in central Europe after that of Prague, established sixteen years earlier. By the middle of the fifteenth century students poured in from all over Europe. Copernicus (1473-1543) has up till now been its most famous son. Doctor Faustus, on whom the main character of Goethe's *Faust* was based, might be placed next.

The living conditions of the Wojtylas in Cracow were unappealing. To quote Blazynski: 'The basement flat at 10 Tynieka Street, which was to be their home in Debniki, was a sad place indeed: hardly any daylight filtered through its narrow windows, the rooms were small and cramped, while the lack of sunshine made the place cold and inhospitable. Locals called it the Debniki "catacomb".'

Wojtyla entered the university in 1938, to study Polish language and literature. From the first, he made his mark as a student among his contemporaries, but by no means limited his interests to the academic curriculum. He enrolled in optional elocution classes. He joined the Polish Language Society. He was quick to join the new theatrical fraternity started in 1938 by some of the writers living in the city. One big production in which he took part was the *Moonlight Cavalier* (1938). It had been especially commissioned by the Theatrical Confraternity, founded by Tadeusz Kydrynski, who was to become an intimate friend of Wojtyla. The play included various figures who represented the powers of the Zodiac, with plenty of satirical references to local persons and events. Pictures of the company show Karol Wojtyla in the role of Sagittarius. Wojtyla was one of four students who not only read out the works of well-known authors, but in addition recited their own poems.

He passed in all subjects with 'credit' in the summer examinations of 1939. Then, on 1 September of that year, the intellectual flowering and the youthful high spirits of Wojtyla and his friends were cruelly cut short. Germany invaded Poland, and within a few months Germany and Russia had completed yet another partition of Poland.

On 1 September 1939, Wojtyla had just made his monthly confession in Wawel Cathedral and was attending Mass. While there, the sound of the first air-raid over Cracow told him that the tragedy for Poland and the world had begun.

The German Army advance into Poland, 1939.

Even today one reads with horror and amazement of the plans of Hitler for Poland, plans put into effect all too efficiently. 'The Poles,' it was laid down by Hitler, 'are especially born for low labour. It is necessary to keep the standard of life low in Poland, and it must not be permitted to rise. The task of a priest is to keep the Poles quiet, stupid and dull-witted.' The Jews were subjected to the most extreme persecution of all.

On 6 November 1939, the professors of the Jagiellonian University in Cracow were invited to hear a lecture in the Collegium Novum on the role of education in the newly partitioned Poland. They attended on the instructions of Dr Hans Frank, head of the German Administration in Poland. Once assembled, all one hundred and eighty-three scholars were promptly arrested and deported to a concentration camp. It was only because of the indignation of Franco, Mussolini and Admiral Horthy of Hungary that many of them were freed after three months in distressing conditions.

In Cracow, as in the rest of Poland, all secondary schools and colleges of higher learning were shut down. The terror increased. Searches, deportations and shootings were continual. The German

43

Institut für Deutsche Ostarbeit, infamous for its criminal activity against Polish learning and culture, arose in the place of the Jagiellonian University.

But this did not mean that Wojtyla had to stop being a student. Underground networks were organized among the few academics who had avoided arrest. Tutorial groups were assembled, classes held in private homes, examinations set and marked. In one way or another, the university's pre-war faculties maintained an active life.

Poster for the play *Knight of the Moon*. Karol Wojtyla *(third from bottom, far right)* performed in this production by Studio 39.

Karol Wojtyla enrolled as a second-year Polish Philology student in a secret cellar within the underground university. He continued also to write poetry.

It was at this time that Wojtyla is said to have formed a sentimental attachment to a young woman. Certainly, like other young men, he had had girlfriends earlier.

The Theatrical Confraternity to which he had belonged before World War II had now gone underground and called itself Studio 39, a reference to the first year of the occupation. Dr Kotlarczyk settled in Cracow in part of the Wojtyla apartment. During the day he was a conductor on a tramway. At night he created the Rhapsodic Theatre. The cast gave 'underground' performances from 1941 to 1945 and the Theatre continued after the war until closed down under the pressure of the new government in 1953. It re-opened in 1957 to be closed down again in 1967. A small, conspiratorial theatrical group was formed of three actresses and two actors, including Wojtyla. Between them they staged five premières and twenty-two performances of plays by famous Polish poets and playwrights, all classics of Polish drama. They met in private apartments before carefully selected audiences. The threat of discovery, with its gloomy consequences, increased if anything the ardour of the survivors. The Secret Police, in a single raid on a rendezvous of intellectuals, had arrested more than two hundred painters, artists and actors, deporting them to Auschwitz.

For Wojtyla, Cyprian Norwid emerged as the most profound of all the Polish poets. It would be Norwid that he would quote most often in later years in his sermons and addresses; in references to work as a way to resurrection, and to the imitation of Christ in the avoidance of slavery.

He underwent during these years another kind of experience vouchsafed to few men of high intellectual calibre and rare indeed among those destined to become ecclesiastical leaders. In 1940 he was sent to hew stones in a quarry belonging to the Solway Chemical Works at Zakrow outside Cracow. Later, he was promoted to assistant shop firer responsible for placing the cartridges and fuses ready for dynamiting the rock, becoming as always during his life a leader among his immediate companions.

In the winter of 1941 he was transferred to the water purification department of the Solway Factory in Borek Falecki, near Cracow. His new job included carrying lime in buckets on a wooden yoke.

These experiences as a proletarian affected his outlook on life. Forty years later he published his encyclical *Laborem exercens*, drafted before the assassination attempt in 1981 and revised while he was recovering. It is the nearest approach to a Hymn to Work and the

Worker that can be conceived of in an encyclical. Its far-reaching application to social and economic policy will be referred to later. But its inspiration must have been drawn directly from those far-off years in the stone quarry. In *Laborem exercens*, John Paul II writes: 'From the beginning man is called to work. Work is one of the characteristics which distinguish man from the rest of the creatures.' John Paul II always looks on work from the point of view of the worker rather than that of the product or the employer. 'The proper subject of work continues to be man.' It is not the size of the product or the efficiency of the operation which is his primary concern, but the quality of the human effort put into it. On this plane, old and young, rich and poor, strong and disabled (to whom he pays special attention), clever and stupid, are all on the same footing.

The connection between work and the family is strongly emphasized. 'Work constitutes a foundation for the formation of family life – the family is simultaneously a community made possible by work and the first school of work within the home for every person.' At the end of the encyclical, work is presented as indissolubly linked

Zakorzowek, the limestone quarry in which Wojtyla worked during the Second World War.

Solway Factory workers read the news of Karol Wojtyla's election to the Papacy in 1978.

with every aspect of life, and with the supreme theological truth of the Cross and Resurrection. The seed planted during the years in the quarry had indeed born abundant fruit.

Pope John Paul II's years at the Solway Factory gave rise to some of his most memorable and most emotive poetry. *The Quarry* was published in November 1957, although Wojtyla had written it in 1956. It is in four parts: 1. Material 2. Inspiration 3. Participation 4. In memory of a fellow worker. The first verse of the first part and particularly its last line gives us a glimpse of the message:

> Listen: the even knocking of hammers,
> so much their own,
> I project on to the people
> to test the strength of each blow.
> Listen now: electric current
> cuts through a river of rock.
> And a thought grown in me day after day:
> the greatness of work is inside man.

The thought is carried on in the second part with lines like these:

> The stone yields you its strength,
> and man matures through work
> which inspires him to difficult good.

In the last part, the just indignation of the exploited worker is transcended and sublimated:

47

Should his anger now flow into the anger of others?
It was maturing in him through its own truth and love.
Should he be used by those who come after,
deprived of substance, unique and deeply his own? . . .
But the man has taken with him the world's inner structure,
where the greater the anger, the higher the explosions of love.

By the time he wrote these words, his intellectual development had carried him far beyond his fellow workers, but his heart would always be with them.

But to return to 1941: in that year, when Karol was only twenty-one, his father died. First his mother, then his only brother, and now his beloved remaining parent. Karol spent a whole night by his father's body. When he emerged, he seemed to be a changed man. Two serious accidents which occurred soon after his father's death affected him deeply. On the first occasion, he was knocked down by

Pope John Paul II kneeling at the family tomb of the Wojtylas at Rakowicki Cemetery in Cracow on his visit to Poland in 1979.

a tram; his skull was fractured. In his delirious state he considered becoming a priest, but when he recovered he decided against it. He was still determined to become a great actor. On the second occasion, a few months later, he narrowly escaped being crushed by a truck. He was left with one shoulder higher than the other, and a permanent stoop. This time he could not resist the call. He joined the illegal theological department of the underground Jagiellonian University.

This decision has been attributed to various influences. The spiritual and religious influence of Jan Tyranowski certainly played a part. Tyranowski was a tailor, an unimposing man with childlike eyes, but he was possessed of a charismatic character and enormous spiritual reserves. In his flat he would organize 'living rosary' circles of which Wojtyla was an active member. Wojtyla was also the Chairman of a Catholic Youth Organization formed by Tyranowski. The organization would meet to discuss religious problems of all kinds and read the works of St John of the Cross.

The appalling treatment of the Jews at the quarry and at the Solway Factory has also been mentioned as an important factor in Wojtyla's decision to enter the priesthood: he was very sympathetic to the predicament of the Jews, and had contributed to resistance work by supplying them with Aryan identification papers. The time spent by his dead father's bedside is regarded by other commentators as being decisive. But one of his oldest friends who knew him well at this time has stressed the importance of the depth of Wojtyla's life of prayer.

In 1944, the German pressure on Poland was intensified. Wojtyla would have been hard put to it to survive if Archbishop Sapieha, who had spotted him at school, had not continued to take a keen interest in him. Adam Sapieha was known as Prince Prince Sapieha because he was a prince by birth and, as Archbishop of Cracow, also a prince of the Church. The Sapiehas were an aristocratic family of orthodox Lithuanian origins. In 1633 Stanislaw Jan Sapieha had obtained the relative dignity of Prince from the Emperor Charles VI. As a student at the Jesuit University of Innsbruck before World War I, Adam Sapieha was one of the young men who arrived in their regional dress with stately retinue and sometimes their own chaplain. But along with his aristocratic outlook on life went a profound care for the poor and for orphaned children. Wojtyla must be thought to owe more to him than to any other single individual.

The authorities did not know of Wojtyla's whereabouts at this time. There were tense moments when Dr Hans Frank visited Sapieha in the course of official duties. He was received with the utmost coldness. The brutality of the occupying power was, if anything, increased after the heroic failure of the Warsaw Uprising in 1944. In January 1945, the Russians swept through Poland providing

a so-called liberation. Wojtyla was free to rejoin the Jagiellonian University.

In August 1946, he took his final examinations in theology. In twenty-six examinations, he achieved the highest possible marks in nineteen, the next highest in six, and the third highest in only one (psychology). On 1 November, Wojtyla was ordained priest by Cardinal Sapieha in his private chapel. All his Cracow and Wadowice friends were present. One of the three Masses which he celebrated on that day in Wawel Cathedral was dedicated to his three closest deceased relatives: his mother, father and brother. On the first Sunday of November, he celebrated the Holy Mass at the parish church in Wadowice. He was twenty-six years of age. The variety of his life before he entered the priesthood had given him a number of advantages over abstract theologians and Bishops who had never, since they left school, been anything but full-time clergymen. The experiences of these years were to prove invaluable to Wojtyla when he became Pope John Paul II.

OPPOSITE Pope John Paul II returns to the font in Wadowice parish church where he was baptized in 1920.

Chapter 3

The Priest and the Scholar 1946–1958

ARCHBISHOP, NOW CARDINAL, SAPIEHA never lost sight of Wojtyla's exceptional promise. He sent Wojtyla to Rome for two years to complete his theological studies. There he lived at the Belgian College, going every day to the Pontifical University of the Angelicum to study philosophy and moral theology. His Director of Studies was the famous French Dominican Garrigou-Lagrange. He had a reputation for die-hard traditionalism, which may have left a permanent mark on Wojtyla, coming as he did from a traditionalist Polish background. There is no doubt that he was overjoyed to find in Lagrange an enthusiast like himself for St John of the Cross. Forty years later, in his *A Sign of Contradiction* Lenten Lectures delivered to Pope Paul VI and the Curia in 1976, Wojtyla quoted lines of St John of the Cross which give us a clue to his own form of mysticism:

'To attain to this which you know not
You must pass through that which you know not.

To attain to this which you possess not
You must pass through that which you possess not.

To attain to this which you are not
You must pass through that which you are not.'

Wojtyla is remembered by various professors and colleagues as having an enormous capacity for work and an ability to reach the centre of any issue under discussion. He could dissect and analyse even the most complex concepts. He did not forget his literary interests in Rome and continued to write poetry. He also showed a gift for establishing contacts and forming friendships with fellow students, regardless of nationality.

Living in the Belgian College meant that he had ample opportunity for acquiring an excellent command of French. It was here that he met the Belgian priest, Fr Marcel Uylenbroeck, the Chaplain General of the *Jeunesse Ouvrière Chrétienne* (Young Christian

OPPOSITE Karol Wojtyla when he was a student

Workers). It stimulated Wojtyla's interest in the problems faced by the working-classes everywhere, an interest which he was never to lose.

It was while he was at the Angelicum that Wojtyla became interested in the philosophy of St Thomas Aquinas. He wrote in a letter to a friend dated 21 January 1947: 'His entire philosophy is so marvellously beautiful, so delightful, and, at the same time, so uncomplicated. It seems that depth of thought does not require a profusion of words. It is even possible that the fewer words there are the deeper the meaning. . . . But I still have far to travel before I hit upon my own philosophy.' Wojtyla pursued his interest in St Thomas Aquinas later in Lublin but it was by no means an exclusive allegiance.

Wojtyla secured a 'licentiate' in 1947. The certificate kept in the archives of the Angelicum shows that he obtained the highest marks possible in the examination. Likewise, when he submitted his thesis entitled *Doctrina de Fide apud S. Joannem de Cruce* (On the doctrine of Faith according to St John of the Cross), he again excelled himself and was awarded nine points out of ten. On 19 June 1948 he became a Doctor of Divinity, *magna cum laude*. The works of St John of the Cross have been a lasting influence in the life of John Paul II. In a talk given to the staff and students of the International College of Discalced Carmelites in Rome on 22 April 1979, John Paul II said, 'I think that in order to understand the dignity and genius of the human person one has to look into the theology of St John of the Cross. His teaching gives us a vision of the nature and meaning of man which will preclude our ever forgetting the value of the human person.'

In Poland, the printing of doctoral theses was forbidden by the Stalinist regime. But the Department of Theology at the Jagiellonian University accepted his thesis, and Wojtyla was again awarded the degree of Doctor of Divinity.

During this period, relations between the Catholic Church and the governing authorities in Poland became increasingly strained. The 1947 elections had been a farce. The political parties had been liquidated, industries and shops nationalized and Church properties confiscated. The so-called Russian 'advisers' were in control, and the country was subjected to an extreme form of Stalinism. By the end of 1948, about four hundred priests were either in prison or in concentration camps in Siberia. Four years later the number had risen to one thousand. To sum it up in Mary Craig's words, 'schools all over the country were being laicized, religious education in schools forbidden, teachers forcibly "re-educated", crucifixes removed, prayers abolished and every religious influence eliminated.'

His ever-helpful patron, Cardinal Sapieha, among others, stood up to the Stalinists boldly. The government hit back at the Catholic

St John of the Cross, the famous sixteenth-century Carmelite mystic

OPPOSITE St Thomas Aquinas in a painting by Filippino Lippi in the Church of Santa Maria Sopra Minerva, Rome

Bishops by accusing them of hostility and treason. The conflict was concentrated on the issue of the Oder-Neisse territories. Pope Pius XII insisted that the territories which had been acquired from Germany did not belong to Poland and he refused to appoint Bishops there. Poland, of course, had been robbed of correspondingly large territories by the Russians. Sapieha did his best to persuade the Pope to appoint Bishops in the Oder-Neisse territories. When he failed, the attitude of the Russian Government became still more unfriendly. Four months later Cardinal Sapieha died. His funeral was one of the most memorable in Polish history.

Things went from bad to worse. The theological department of the Jagiellonian was closed down again (and remains closed today). Although several seminaries stayed open, higher theological studies were allowed only in the independent Catholic University of Lublin (KUL) and in the new Academy of Catholic Theology set up in Warsaw. The Academy was the equivalent of a university, with the lecturers being paid by the State.

The government continued to support so-called 'patriotic' priests, loyal to the State. They imposed a ban on all Catholic organizations and refused to allow a ration of newsprint to the genuine Catholic publications.

The newly appointed Archbishop of Warsaw, Stefan Wyszynski wrote to President Bierut accusing the government of bad faith in its dealings with the Church. He also attempted to persuade the Vatican to appoint residential Bishops in the Oder-Neisse territories, but, like Sapieha, he failed. At a press conference in Rome he complained, 'You talk about the Church of Silence, but here in Rome it is the Church of the Deaf.' In the circumstances, it was not difficult for the government to accuse him of betraying Poland's interests.

The new Polish Constitution of 1952 guaranteed freedom of conscience and belief to all citizens, but this was a living lie. Seminaries were being closed throughout the land and most of the students sent to labour camps. By the end of 1952 over eight Bishops and nine hundred priests, among them Archbishop Baziak, the Apostolic Administrator and Wojtyla's superior, were in prison. The protests of the Primate were counter-productive. In 1953 came the show trial of Bishop Kaczmarek. He had been held in prison for thirty-two months, and was finally pressurized into accusing himself of all sorts of crimes against the State. Cardinal Wyszynski vehemently protested and was, in consequence, relieved of his functions and placed under arrest. Wojtyla, not yet a Bishop, managed to avoid imprisonment and he concentrated on pastoral affairs, although in 1953 he began to lecture in secret at the banned Metropolitan Seminary in Cracow in moral theology and social ethics.

OPPOSITE Pope John Paul II with Cardinal Stefan Wyszynski, Primate of Poland

Stalin died in 1953, but his influence continued to be felt. However, living conditions in Poland had become so intolerable that, in June 1956, 16,000 workers from the Cegielski Factory in Poznan demonstrated in the streets for bread and freedom. On 15 August at the Feast of the Assumption, a million and a half people converged on Czestochowa to petition the Virgin Mary for an end to the oppression and for the release of Cardinal Wyszynski. Eventually Mr Gomulka, the Prime Minister, released the Cardinal from prison. The Cardinal appealed to the Polish Catholics for loyalty to the Republic.

An agreement was drawn up that Bishops and priests were to be released from prison; religious instruction was to be reinstated; freedom and tolerance were to be restored. The Church agreed, for the first time, to recognize the existing political situation and to accept its economic basis. In Poland this looked like a satisfactory arrangement for the Church, but Pope Pius was anything but pleased. When Cardinal Wyszynski went to Rome to explain the advantages of the new arrangement, Pope Pius XII kept him waiting for several days before granting him an audience. However, a new era of reconciliation between Church and State lasted, however precariously, for the next few years.

Meanwhile, Wojtyla had established himself as an unforgettable priest. Many admired the extreme simplicity of his life. He was sent first as curate to the little village of Niegowic, near Cracow. He arrived on foot on 18 July 1948, and years later Stanislaw Substelny was to recall his first meeting with Wojtyla. 'He was walking from Gdow. He wore shabby trousers, a waistcoat, worn-out shoes, and carried a briefcase that I would be ashamed to take with me to market. He asked me the quickest way to Niegowic. I asked him why he wanted to go there, and he answered that he was going to work in the parish. He went away and knelt before a wayside shrine which still stands there today. He prayed for a long time and then he got up and went the way I told him.'

Wojtyla spent little more than a year in Niegowic. But in that time he became beloved of his poor congregation. There was a woman called Tadeuscka, who once came to see Fr Wojtyla to complain that she had been robbed. He gave her what he had, even a pillow and eiderdown. This kind of self-sacrifice, so close to the spirit of the Gospel, was not universally popular. His people had just bought him the pillow and eiderdown because he slept on bare boards. They wished that he would be a little less generous with their presents to him.

At Christmastime it was a custom for each family to give some money to the Church. Fr Wojtyla gave the money to the poor but

The parish church at Niegowic where Karol Wojtyla was sent as a curate in 1948.

he himself had no personal belongings, so girls from the Catholic Youth Association sewed a feather quilt for him. He accepted it gratefully, then offered it to three of the girls whose mother had recently died.

His permanent memorial at Niegowic is the local church. It contains a plaque which boasts that it was built by voluntary efforts that were initiated by Karol Wojtyla. To mark the fiftieth anniversary of the ministry of the parish priest, a meeting was held and various possibilities considered. Someone suggested painting the boarding round the old church. But Wojtyla was never one for half measures. 'Why not,' he said, 'build a new church?' There was much sadness when he was moved after a year to the substantial parish of St Florian's in Cracow. But the villagers had realized that they were unlikely to keep their exceptional priest for very long.

The curate Wojtyla with his
altar boys

Wojtyla arrived at St Florian's in a rickety old peasant cart drawn
by one horse, carrying a small case and a few books. At first there
was some doubt as to whether his obvious poverty was a point in his
favour. His cassock, faded and threadbare, was felt to be a disgrace.
The parishioners persuaded the parish priest to order Fr Wojtyla to
accept a new overcoat as well, although he never wore it. Gradually
these eccentricities endeared him to everyone.

Wojtyla's eloquence in the pulpit drew large congregations, at-
tracting even those who were indifferent to religion. Though some
members of his congregation found them too long, his sermons
were generally compact and expertly delivered, and he modulated
his voice dextrously to underline the main theme of the sermon.
Those sermons on the problems of Christian ethics provoked special
interest, although the solutions he put forward were far from accept-
able to the majority of the listeners. He stressed that spiritual growth
and self-realization were to be found through Christian asceticism
and renunciation.

As a curate, Wojtyla organized a group of young acolytes using
unorthodox methods of education and training, based on modern

teaching principles. He was popular with the young people, and he would frequently play football with them on a common near Cracow. Bearing in mind the Stalinists' attitude towards the Catholics at the time, such behaviour reflects Wojtyla's personal courage. Indeed, many priests had been arrested for similar activities.

In his spare time, Wojtyla jotted down ideas for plays, for he was still greatly attracted by the theatre. One of the plays focused on the Polish painter, Brother Albert, who gave up his art to serve the poor and the disinherited. In 1950 *Tygodnik Powszechny*, the heavily censored weekly newspaper, published some of his poems, under a pseudonym, for the first time.

In 1951 he was released from pastoral duties to undertake further academic studies. The moving spirit here was his former professor at the theological department of the Jagiellonian University, Fr Rozycki, who must be credited with recognizing in Wojtyla an unusual philosophic talent. Rozycki approached the then Archbishop of Cracow, Baziak. He obtained for Wojtyla a dispensation from parish work for the time being, on condition that he took up residence with his professor in Cracow. He would stay there for six years from 1952 to 1958, when he was made an Auxiliary Bishop. All through this time Rozycki was able to nurse Wojtyla's intellectual development. Wojtyla read widely in personalism, existentialism and, particularly, phenomenology, which is based on the study of the *object*, that is to say reality, what is already there. He studied, among many other works, those of Max Buber, Gabriel Marcel, and above all Max Scheler. Wojtyla was already at home in the German language through the Silesian ancestry of his mother, the Austrian military career of his father, and his own five years under Nazi occupation in Poland.

Max Scheler had a strange career. He is often referred to as a pupil of Edmund Husserl, the founder of phenomenology, though Husserl came to disown him. Scheler was born in Munich, the son of a Lutheran bailiff and a Jewish mother. At the age of fourteen, Scheler broke with the Jewish religion of his mother and was baptized as a Catholic. He soon made his mark as a brilliant young teacher, but he was deprived of his right to teach at Munich for moral turpitude. It was after this that he settled in Göttingen close to Husserl. His Catholic period, which began actively in 1912, did not last beyond 1922. The break with Catholicism was connected with his second divorce and third marriage, but he could supply theoretical reasons for the changes in his beliefs. It was the writings of Scheler's Catholic phase that influenced the future Pope.

When Wojtyla began his studies in 1951, his original purpose was to reconcile other philosophical ideas with the traditional teaching of St Thomas Aquinas. His thesis was entitled 'The Possibilities of Building a System of Christian Ethics on the Basis of Max Scheler'. Although his conclusions were not in sympathy with Scheler, he always acknowledged his debt to Scheler's method. The thesis earned him another doctorate. He was now uniquely equipped as theologian and philosopher.

By October 1953, Wojtyla was lecturing on social ethics at the Cracow Theological Seminary. He obviously revelled in the university atmosphere of Cracow where he himself had been a student. The new generation of students came to call him 'the eternal teenager' but his powerful intellect was being noticed in wider circles. In 1956 he was offered the Chair of Ethics in Lublin University. Unlike any other city in Eastern Europe, Lublin has a Catholic University, wholly supported by donations from clerical and lay sources. Before being appointed professor, he had been tried out as a lecturer and found more than satisfactory. By the age of thirty-six he had acquired the full status of a professor and was head of the Institute of Ethics at Lublin.

But there was no question of his giving up his pastoral duties among the university students in Cracow, where attendance at his lectures grew continually. He regularly commuted by overnight train between Cracow and Lublin, a distance of about one hundred and fifty miles. His eloquence was equally admired by students in both cities.

Wojtyla did not cease to be a professor when he became a Bishop. His interest in technical philosophy never flagged. His main philosophical work, *The Acting Person*, was not published until 1969 and was translated into English, much revised, in 1979. In the meantime he had taken part in a number of international conferences which discussed phenomenology in particular. He specifically states that *The Acting Person* is not an ethical treatise. But one passage bearing on ethics must be referred to. He takes up the commandment 'Thou shalt love thy neighbour as thyself' and uses it to confirm the outcome of his phenomenological investigations. They go far to demonstrate that 'the mutual relation and subordination of all men according to the principle of their common humanness' brings us by a different route to the same conclusion as the second commandment.

Today, there might seem to be political implications in this severely philosophical volume. These were no doubt present in the author's mind, but were likely to arouse less attention then than they do in the 1980s. Wojtyla insists that people can only realize themselves fully within the structure of a community and suggests that 'both solidarity and opposition are needed as necessary components if persons are to be fulfilled'. 'Solidarity' today has a more militant

OPPOSITE Pope John Paul II mingles with students on his visit to Poland in 1979.

Wojtyla on an outing with a group of children when he was Bishop of Cracow

implication than can have been intended when he was writing in the 1950s. Wojtyla is pointing to the double duty falling to the lot of Poles: on the one hand to play their full part in the State as they find it; on the other, to stand firm for religious and other principles which no tyranny can ever abolish.

Some will feel that his deepest thoughts were expressed during these years in poetry. One striking example of this has already been seen in *The Quarry*. It may at first appear surprising that a theologian and philosopher should also feel the need to express himself in poetry. But, bearing in mind that Wojtyla's original purpose for enrolling at university was to read Polish language and literature, then poetry can be seen as an extension of this fascination with language. Even in translation, the reader can detect the pleasure derived by the poet from playing with words.

His work was originally published under the pseudonym 'Jawien', and it was not until Wojtyla was elected Pope that the poet's true identity became known. The poems mirror the poet's own spiritual development and stem from the days of the Communist attack on religion in Poland in the 1950s, through the time spent by Wojtyla in the Episcopal Palace in Cracow and in Rome for Vatican Council

II, to 1966, when Poland celebrated one thousand years of Christianity. His poems deal with the concrete rather than abstract forms of man's spirituality and frequently dwell on physical features like the hands, eyes and face. As he wrote in *The Birth of the Confessors*, 'The shape of the face says everything/Where else such expression of being?'

His choice of subject is all-embracing, ranging from the religious where he writes about the Virgin Mary, affectionately referred to as 'Mother', Simon of Cyrene, and Mary Magdalene, to the more prosaic where his subjects include the car factory worker and a typist. For men of all ages, he shows compassion and understanding. He speaks, for example, of children with concern, saying, 'The pulse of mankind beats in their hearts' and fears for their corruption, wondering if they will 'always separate the right from the wrong'. This concern and love for children was seen particularly clearly on his tours as Pope. He took great delight in the children presented to him or those he glimpsed with their parents among the crowds.

Some of the poems contain a didactic element and point to the danger of alienating oneself through leaning towards extremes. Indeed, if ever there were a good example of the perfect balance of heart and head, Wojtyla surely supplies it.

The importance of balance is emphasized by the image of the scales in several of his poems. Although Wojtyla points to God as the solution to our mundane problems, the general tone of his poems is by no means complacent. In some he is anxious; in others uncertain. Yet in his later poem, *The Birth of the Confessors*, the first section of which is called 'A Bishop's thoughts on giving the sacrament of confirmation in a mountain village', the poet's voice is confident, and his lines almost prophetic as he writes:

> The world is charged with hidden energies
> and boldly I call them by name . . .
> I am a giver, I touch forces that expand the mind.

Is this how he sees his role in the Church today? Indeed, if we, like the individual in *Words' Resistance to Thought*, 'tear through the thicket of signs/ to the word's very centre' in order to learn more of the man who wrote the poetry, we are given invaluable insights into the man behind the name John Paul II.

Chapter 4

Totus Tuus
1958-1978

WOJTYLA RECEIVED THE NEWS that Pope Pius XII had appointed him Auxiliary Bishop of Cracow on 4 July 1958 when he was on a canoeing holiday with students in Mazuria. Wojtyla was summoned to Warsaw by the Primate of Poland, Cardinal Wyszynski, and he was carried shoulder high by his pupils to the bus which was to take him back to the city. On 28 September, he was consecrated Bishop in Wawel Cathedral in Cracow. He wrote on his Bishop's seal the Latin words, *Totus Tuus* (All Yours). Twenty years later in his first papal message, *Urbi et Orbi*, he said, 'At this very difficult hour, full of fear, we must turn our thoughts with filial devotion to the Virgin Mary who always lives in the midst of Christ, and exists as his mother. We must repeat the words *Totus Tuus* which twenty years ago on the day of our consecration as Bishop were inscribed into our heart and soul.'

The next twenty years saw Karol Wojtyla progress steadily from Auxiliary Bishop to Pope. In the wordly sense, the key dates are 1964, when he was consecrated Archbishop of Cracow; 1967, when he was created Cardinal; and 1978, which saw his election as Pope.

Although he did not give up teaching, Wojtyla's duties as Bishop of Cracow made it increasingly difficult for him to go to Lublin so often. But however busy he was, he tried to fit in meetings with his students and academic assistants. He wanted to find time for everything and everyone. Once, he performed a wedding ceremony in a little country church in the mountains at 7 a.m. on a Monday morning because this was the only hour at which he had time to spare. Although he was known to all as 'Uncle', no one learned as much about him as he learned about them. He was much more interested in hearing about other people than in talking about himself.

Meanwhile his academic publications continued. His pupils learned that writing a PhD was only one of the qualifications needed to become his academic assistant. The ideal assistant had, in addition, to know German and to be able to ski. One assistant who was unable to ski played volleyball and went canoeing with him.

Love and Responsibility was first published in Polish in 1960, and

OPPOSITE *Totus Tuus*, the motto of Pope John Paul II, was chosen by him when he became a Bishop in 1958 and remains his personal emblem today.

Wojtyla loved the
countryside around Cracow.
He relaxed by canoeing,
cycling and, in the winter,
skiing in the Tatras
Mountains.

translated into English in 1981. In it, philosophy and theology are combined in a way for which it would be difficult to find a recent parallel.

This is indeed a book about love, and no one has more right to speak on that subject than Pope John Paul II, but it is also concerned with the implications of love and with what John Paul II calls 'the personalistic norm'. Again, the emphasis is on the sentiments of the second commandment, 'Thou shalt love thy neighbour as thyself'; a human person should never be used as a means to an end but always treated as an end in him or herself. His objection to artificial birth control is based on his writings in *Love and Responsibility*. 'The specific characteristic of the human person is the ability to fit the order of nature into the framework of the personal order.' For him, the safe period is in accordance with the order of nature. Artificial birth control violates it. Nature to him has behind it the personal authority of the Creator.

Wojtyla's whole life was changed by the Second Vatican Council, summoned by Pope John XXIII in 1959 and meeting for the first time in 1962. It broadened the horizons of this young religious leader from Poland and led him to consider the wider role of the Church in the world. He was totally committed to the aims of the Vatican Council. He spoke on 7 November 1962 on the liturgy, and on 21 November on the sources of revelation. On 23 September 1963, he urged that the Church should be seen as the 'people of God', and that the Church as a whole must take precedence over the hierarchy, the whole coming before its parts. By the end of the Council in 1965 he had already exerted a considerable influence.

Two of the most important documents which emerged from the Council were *Lumen Gentium* (21 November 1964) and *Gaudium et Spes* (7 December 1965). It will never be known exactly how much the present Pope contributed to these documents, but it would seem that his influence was important in each case and particularly in the final version of *Gaudium et Spes*. It may well be asked how it was that someone who only became a young Auxiliary Bishop in 1958 and did not receive further preferment until he became Archbishop of Cracow in 1964 came to play such a crucial part in the Council. There seems no doubt about the answer. Someone very close to Wojtyla at that time has told me that he, Wojtyla, was 'discovered' by Pope Paul VI. He was given his chance to influence the whole history of the Church and grasped it with both hands.

There is only room here for the briefest of quotations from each document. In *Lumen Gentium* we read that, 'the universal church is seen to be a *people* [my italics] brought into unity from the unity of the Father, the son and the Holy Spirit. . . . As all the members of the

A room in the Episcopal Palace, Cracow

human body, though they are many, form one body, so are the faithful in Christ [i.e. laity as well as clergy]. . . . Though they differ essentially and not only in degree, the common priesthood of the faithful and the ministerial or hierarchical priesthood are nonetheless orders one to another; each in its own way shares in the one *priesthood* [again, my italics].' *Gaudium et Spes* refers to the joy and hope, the grief and the anguish, which the followers of Christ share with all men and women. They, the followers of Christ, press onwards towards the kingdom of the Father and are the bearers of the message of salvation for *all men* [my italics].

It has been said that Wojtyla was on the side of those who favoured a more biblical and less clerical approach to the Church. Those like Archbishop Worlock who later sat with the present Pope for many years on the Laity Council would be inclined to stress his special sense of the dignity of 'man', that is all men, in his approach to the laity. In later contributions, Wojtyla drew on his special experience of life under Communist domination.

At this period, and indeed later, it would be far too simple to speak of him as having adopted a conservative versus liberal point of view.

72

In the early days of the Council there were plenty of conservatives who thought that the declarations of religious liberty conceded too much to 'error'. Wojtyla pointed out persuasively that the Church could only claim religious liberty where it was weak, for example in Eastern Europe, if it was prepared to concede it in the countries where it was strong.

The simple bedroom of Bishop Wojtyla in the Episcopal Palace

Wojtyla's lifestyle was certainly quite different from that of a traditional Bishop, Archbishop or Cardinal. It remained unchanged in spirit throughout the next twenty years following his appointment as Bishop but, when he became Archbishop of Cracow in 1964, he was persuaded, with difficulty, to abandon his two-roomed flat and to move into the old Episcopal Palace at No. 3 Franciszkanska Street. But even in those august surroundings he continued to live in a very simple style.

From the splendour of the Palace Hall, as George Blazynski has noted, you enter a cramped corridor with a staircase which is in need of fresh paint. 'Wojtyla's quarters comprised a small entrance hall, a large study and a tiny bedroom. Here stands a simple desk with peeling varnish and some papers, a simple bed with a worn bedspread covering it, and a colourful pillow with some gay folk decorations. On the wall hang a Renaissance Madonna and a Polish winter landscape. On his bedside table lies a rosary next to a Thermos flask and glass. On the floor and just under the bed, are a pair of used black shoes. Everything was always in its proper place.' The room is just as he left it when he went to Rome in October 1978.

A servant at the Palace recalls that in the days of Cardinal Sapieha he had 'a lot of free time'. But when Wojtyla was made Archbishop the residence was filled with people from morning to night. Wojtyla never had his meals alone. From the beginning he announced that the Palace was to be open to the public. He got up at 5 o'clock. At 7 o'clock, he celebrated Mass and then ate breakfast with his staff. He worked by himself until 11 o'clock, when he held audiences until late in the afternoon. His last guests would be offered dinner. A short walk was fitted in, then supper which was followed by more guests. The lights went out at midnight. But in the chapel Wojtyla prayed on and on. This routine was frequently disturbed by his pastoral visitations, episcopal conferences, and trips abroad. 'Uncle's friends' often numbered as many as two hundred when they came

Wojtyla's study in the Bishop's Palace, Cracow

with their children. The constant stream of visitors which included doctors, workers, artists, priests and nuns, increased uncontrollably.

When Wojtyla became a Cardinal in May 1967, an old fellow pupil from Wadowice High School was with him. The Cardinal was being congratulated by all. His old schoolfriend began his own congratulations with the words, 'Your Eminence . . .' but the Cardinal stopped him. 'Jurek, have you taken leave of your senses?'

Wojtyla never stopped reading books in many languages, but felt that radio and television were 'a waste of time'. His office was open every day from 11 a.m. to 1 p.m. to anyone who wanted to come and see him. He worked tirelessly for anything up to twenty hours a day. But his love of skiing never left him, whether in Poland or Italy.

When Wojtyla was appointed Archbishop, he took his skis and canoeing paddles with him to the Palace in Cracow. Usually he went on camping holidays with a group of young people. Sometimes he would go on holiday with a few intellectual friends. On one occasion, however, he stayed at a rest home for young priests in the Tatras mountains. An elderly priest, not knowing that Wojtyla was a Cardinal, used him for small personal errands such as fetching tea. Wojtyla performed all these services without demur. It was not till much later that the elderly priest learned that his young acolyte was, in fact, a Cardinal. Stories of this kind illustrate a humility which is rare indeed among the great ones of the earth.

A friend describes Wojtyla as 'one of the daredevils' as a skier. When he discovered that none of the Italian Cardinals skied, Wojtyla remarked: 'That's strange. In Poland, forty per cent of all our Cardinals are skiers.' With only two Polish Cardinals, the implication that Wyszynski represented sixty per cent was easily appreciated. Someone once asked him whether it was becoming for a Cardinal to ski. His answer was, 'It is unbecoming for a Cardinal to ski badly.' There is another well-known story about Wojtyla as a skier. Once he was skiing near the Czechoslovakian border and was stopped by a militia patrol. The militiaman to whom Wojtyla showed his identity card did not recognize the Cardinal, dressed as he was in his skiing outfit, and grunted: 'Do you realize, you moron, whose personal papers you have stolen? This trick will put you inside for a long time.' When Wojtyla tried to explain that he was indeed a Cardinal, the militiaman shouted: 'A skiing Cardinal! Do you think I'm nuts?' Later he was suitably apologetic.

Wojtyla enjoyed all forms of sport on the mountains, however bad the conditions. When mountain climbing the Cardinal, with his iron constitution, could put to shame even the younger men. When the weather was so bad that the ski lifts were not working, the Cardinal used to say to one of his assistants: 'There won't be anybody on the mountain today, let's go and try it.' In the vivid words of Tadeusz Karolak, 'The wind overwhelmed them, and they held onto stones because snow swept over them, and the wind whipped at them, blinding them.' We are told that the Cardinal relaxed at such times and when he returned, 'he was completely changed'. Not everyone's form of enjoyment, but he drew from it unfailing strength.

When Wojtyla was made a Cardinal, there were those who thought that it was intended that he should act as a sort of balance to Cardinal Wyszynski, the indomitable hard-liner. There were important points of contrast between the two, apart from the fact that Wojtyla was twenty years younger than Wyszynski. As a church leader, Wojtyla welcomed the second Vatican Council wholeheartedly, while Wyszynski remained suspicious.

Cardinal Wyszynski appeared beyond question to be a conservative and a traditionalist. The words have been applied to the present Pope quite often since that time, but there can be no doubt that they give a much truer description of Wyszynski. There were a number of Polish Catholic intellectual groups who looked on Cardinal Wojtyla as a potential protector. They certainly had never any cause to find him wanting in this respect, but he was careful to act in a manner which would not offend Cardinal Wyszynski. When General de Gaulle visited Poland in 1967, he was persuaded by the Polish government to abandon his original intention of meeting the Polish Primate. Cardinal Wojtyla saw to it that he, himself, was otherwise engaged when de Gaulle arrived in Cracow. Such acts of loyalty and deference were not motivated only by a sense of propriety. Wojtyla has given evidence of loving Wyszynski, as a son loves a father.

On receiving the news of his appointment as Cardinal, Wojtyla dropped everything and rushed to Warsaw to report to Wyszynski and receive his congratulations. When he returned to Cracow, welcomed by thousands of rejoicing crowds who showered him with flowers, he paid his 'most reverent homage' to the Primate. 'He had brought,' Wojtyla said, 'a kiss from the Pope and that admiration which he enjoys in the whole of Christ's Church and all over the world for his unbreakable power of spirit.'

These were not mere words. Nor did anyone ever suppose they were. Wyszynski himself knew that they came from the depths of a full heart. And he amply reciprocated the sentiment. After Wojtyla had been elected Pope, he had this to say: 'When he has a mission to fulfil he does it with the simplicity of a son of the Polish nation who knows only one word to say to God: Yes!'

OPPOSITE Wojtyla reading his breviary during a skiing trip to the Tatras Mountains.

The Cardinal elect receives his Cardinal's biretta from Pope Paul VI.

Wojtyla attended four of the five Synods which took place between 1967 and 1977. Neither he nor any of the other Polish Bishops attended the first Synod held in 1967. He had been one of five Bishops elected to represent the Polish Episcopate, but when Cardinal Wyszynski and another Bishop were refused permission to leave the country, Cardinal Wojtyla and the remaining members of the delegation declined to leave Poland. The Episcopate, in a communiqué read in all churches, accused the authorities of seriously restricting the freedom of religion. It was revealed that the Primate had been refused permission to travel almost at the last minute. But at the other Synods, Wojtyla increasingly made his unmistakeable mark.

In 1963 Pope John XXIII had set up a Commission to study and report on the question of artificial birth control. At the end of June 1964, Pope Paul VI enlarged the Commission. Archbishop Wojtyla was appointed at the fifth session, which met in April 1966. A majority report did not uphold the Church's provisional total ban on all forms of artificial contraception. A minority report advocated a maintenance of the *status quo*. Archbishop Wojtyla was absent from the meeting at which the crucial vote was taken, but there is no doubt that he would have voted on the conservative side of the argument, in accordance with his known views.

As we all know by now, Pope Paul VI set aside the majority opinion, for good or for ill. Cardinal (as he was by now) Wojtyla

OPPOSITE Cardinal Wojtyla

clearly approved the Pope's decision. He suggested that the Third World was mostly in agreement with him, and that the main opposition came from wealthy nations. In recommending the final declaration of the Synod on 27 October 1969, Cardinal Wojtyla adopted a tone of loyalty and pacification. 'In our days,' he said, 'during which storms are invading the Church and the world, there is nothing more important than the testimony of union and the spreading of peace. This union in the Church which is desired so ardently by the Christian people depends very largely on the collaboration both between the Supreme Pontiff and the Bishops' conference and between the conferences among themselves.'

In 1971, Wojtyla spoke on 'the serving priesthood' and 'justice in the world' drawing emphatically on his Polish experience. The State, he said, favours all the organizations which support atheism in order to give expression to the programme of anti-Catholicism of the secular world. The Church knew its task was to preserve spiritual values and make no concession to atheism. Not for the first or last time, Wojtyla insisted that celibacy was essential if a priest were to give himself entirely to the service of others. On the subject of justice in the world, he proclaimed that without real freedom there could be no real justice. It was in this year that he was elected to the permanent Council of the Synod. He came ninth in the voting, though still relatively young.

In 1974, he came fourth in the ballot, one of only two Europeans in the first ten. At this Synod he was appointed *Rapporteur* of the second part of the proceedings. The subject was 'The Gospel in the Modern World'. He produced a paper on the theological implications of re-evangelization which Dr Thomas Holland, Bishop of Salford, described as 'a towering massive piece of theological reflection carrying certain issues further than I have ever seen them taken'. It was a major theological event of the last decade. The young Pole, ordained at the age of twenty-six, with little formal education, had become a leading intellectual force in world Catholicism.

One or two of the main points which he made at that time must be mentioned. Authentic evangelization can only be referred to when what is proclaimed and talked about is exclusively the Gospel of Jesus Christ, and not human opinions. But he was then, as always, in favour of dialogue, something which, as a Professor of Ethics in a Communist-ruled country, he had exceptional experience of. Dialogue, he insisted, presupposes certainty in the faith, without admitting any kind of conformism or doctrinal indifference. Although in multilateral dialogue there is room for a certain opening of the human spirit, individual faith must never be whittled down or weakened.

OPPOSITE Cardinal Wojtyla in the Vatican with Pope Paul VI

81

Surely we are close here to one of the secrets of his immense appeal, not only to Catholics but to all members of the Christian religion, and even to atheists. There is the rock-like certainty about the truth of his own position, but a readiness to listen to others, not patronizingly but from a deep-rooted conviction that every human being has something of the divine within him or her.

The 1977 Synod dealt with the problem of religious education. In the absence of Cardinal Wyszynski, Cardinal Wojtyla led the Polish delegation. He dealt severely with Marxist attacks on the Church: 'Atheism is being imposed like a new religion.' The Polish authorities were discriminating against Christians in public life, and prohibiting religious instruction in Polish schools. As the most senior Cardinal on the Council of the Synod's Secretariat, Cardinal Wojtyla became Chairman. By this time, he was a member of several important Congregations which included the Congregation for the Eastern Churches; for the clergy; for divine service and Catholic education; and for the liturgy. He was also consultant to the Papal Council for members of the lay apostolate. He was becoming a more and more significant figure in Rome although he was well content to remain the second Polish Cardinal.

As government restrictions on travel outside Poland became more relaxed, Cardinal Wojtyla began to tour abroad more and more, setting the pattern that the world was to come to know so well when he was elected Pope. He was anxious to attend Church ceremonies, meet foreign religious dignitaries, and particularly to re-establish contact with Poles who were now living abroad. He attended the Australian Ecumenical Congress in 1970 and stopped on his way back in New Guinea where, in the words of Peter Hebblethwaite, that expert in Catholic affairs, 'He was delightfully photographed among feathered warriors'. He made his first visit to North America and Canada in August 1969. He visited Montreal, Quebec and Ottawa, Toronto, Hamilton, St Catherine's and London, Winnipeg, Calgary and Edmonton. In the United States, he concentrated on such places of importance as Polish settlements or important Marian shrines which included Baltimore, Boston and Chicago, Detroit, New York and Philadelphia. As time went on, he became increasingly well known on that side of the Atlantic.

In 1973, he returned to Australia to attend the Eucharistic Congress there and visited New Zealand and the Philippines. In 1976, he attended a Eucharistic Congress in Philadelphia. He never for a moment forgot his home country, and always made particular efforts to meet Poles wherever he visited. In Chicago he was twice seen strolling round Polish neighbourhoods. In Philadelphia the Polish Episcopate was represented by a delegation of eighteen Bishops

OPPOSITE Pope John Paul II praying before a portrait of the Blessed Maximilian Kolbe. On his visit to Auschwitz, the Pope talked about the inspiration of the strength of Kolbe's faith.

under his leadership. Cardinal Wojtyla took a leading part. Services were carried out before thousands of assembled pilgrims, sometimes assisted by as many as five hundred concelebrants. Always the spiritual came first with him. But his intellectual energy was exercised repeatedly. Before the Philadelphia celebrations, for example, he gave three lectures for English-speaking audiences in Wisconsin on the state of Polish religious scholarship; at Harvard, on participation or alienation; and at the Catholic University of America, on his own particular brand of personalism. He had at the same time widespread contacts with the Church in Africa and corresponded widely with black Bishops and missionaries. He was frequently visited in Cracow by Cardinals and Bishops from many countries.

Between 1958 and 1978 relations between the Catholic leaders in Poland and the Communist authorities went through many ups and downs, more downs than ups. In 1966, two years after Wojtyla became Archbishop of Cracow, there came the celebration of one thousand years of Polish Christianity. It was the brainchild of Cardinal Wyszynski, who throughout this period was Wojtyla's superior. From year to year sermons and Catholic apologetics had been developed to make all Catholics aware of their responsibility. In Peter Hebblethwaite's words, 'It was an act of outright defiance to the Government. The churches, by declaring that our Lady was "Queen of Poland" were declaring at the same time that she was the true sovereign of Poland and that, therefore, the current relations of the country were temporarily superfluous.'

The government did all it could to sabotage the celebrations. It is possible that Wojtyla would have preferred to fight and so trigger a confrontation, but at all times he settled for the unity of the Polish Episcopate. Any attempt on the part of the government to divide him from Wyszynski was doomed to failure.

There was one local issue of national significance where the Church made it clear that they would not give in. Four miles from Cracow is the steel town of Nowa Huta. It was a new town intended during the Stalinist period to be a trial home for the new Socialist mayor. In 1957, the authorities agreed under considerable pressure to the siting of a church there, but in 1960 they changed their mind and workers were sent to remove the cross which had been set up as a symbol. There were pitched battles in the streets of Nowa Huta. Eventually the authorities relented and the task of building a church in Nowa Huta could begin.

The building of the church started on 14 October 1967 when at 7 a.m. Cardinal Wojtyla arrived at the town. He celebrated Holy Mass, wielded a pickaxe, and dug the first section of the trench in the foundations with a spade. From that day onwards, hundreds of

people came every day to help build the church. The Cardinal took
the keenest interest at all times. Under his encouragement, young
people worked during their holidays, with the idea that it was pay-
ment for the crime perpetrated by Nazis during World War II on
Polish territory. The Cardinal loved to come and visit the young
workers and joined in their discussions, their jokes and songs. He
placed the corner stone in the wall with his own hands, dedicated the
walls and was present at the placing of the roof and the raising of
the cross. At last, on 15 May 1977, the church was consecrated. In
his sermon on that day, he delivered this message: 'A church is not
merely a building; it is made up of living stones. This was built as a
city without God, but the will of God and the people who work
here has prevailed. Let this be a lesson.'

Cardinal Wojtyla addressing
the congregation at the
consecration of the church at
Nowa Huta, 1977.

85

The Pope returns to the church of Nowa Huta on his tour of Poland in 1979.

In the crypt of the church stands the massive statue of the blessed Father Maximilian Kolbe in his striped prison clothes, the priest who gave his life in martyrdom in the death camp at Auschwitz so that the father of a family might be saved. Time and again, in one context or another, Wojtyla returns to the example of Kolbe. The church at Nowa Huta is also a symbol of Polish–German reconciliation, for the German Christian Movement contributed to its building.

1968 was a year of revolutionary student action all over Europe and America. There were student uprisings, mild or not so mild, even in Britain. In January 1968 in Poland a play called *Ancestors* by by Adam Miciewicz was staged in Cracow and Warsaw. It had been written as a protest against early nineteenth-century Russian atrocities. In Poland, *Ancestors* met with colossal enthusiasm from Polish students and intellectuals, but was soon taken off. A few weeks later students and intellectuals demonstrated on the streets demanding an end to censorship, but the workers did not feel that this was their quarrel, and held back. The government reckoned that the students and intellectuals could be easily subdued if they had no active support, and acted with brutal effectiveness, sacking and arresting

OPPOSITE The Pope looks into a cell at Auschwitz.

John Paul II with the then
First Secretary of the Polish
Upper Worker's Party,
Edward Gierek

academics and expelling students. Many of the disaffected academics
were Jewish, and the government began an anti-Semitic purge.
Although Wojtyla persuaded his fellow Bishops to speak up for the
unfortunate Jews, the Church in Poland, collectively speaking,
refused to become involved in the conflict. The students and intellectuals had criticized them sharply over the years. This, said the
Church, was a family quarrel between Communists. Wojtyla alone
spoke out boldly in defence of the students, whom he knew so well.

There have continued to be many confrontations between Church
and State. Just before Christmas 1969, Gomulka raised food prices
by almost twenty-five per cent, while wages and salaries remained
static. The workers erupted in widespread violence. Police resorted
to gunfire, and hundreds of workers were killed. It resulted in
Gomulka's fall from power. When the new Party Secretary, Edward
Gierek, took over, the riots continued until he was forced to give
way. Gierek's Prime Minister, Jaroszewicz, seemed to have learned
something of a lesson from all this. In his first speech to the Polish
parliament, Jaroszewicz said that the government wished to strength-
en cooperation between all citizens in Poland, whether believers or
non-believers. He hoped that this policy would meet with understanding from Catholic clergy and laity.

The Church in Poland has been strongly influenced by Wojtyla
and has shown a willingness to sustain a dialogue with the Communists, provided that they accord the Church the freedom it is
seeking. In all these matters, friendly relations with the West German
hierarchy were essential, and these Cardinal Wojtyla did much to
foster.

The Pope relaxing in song with clerical students on his Polish visit.

In 1977, the year before he was elected Pope, tension mounted in Poland. A group of hunger strikers took possession of a church in Warsaw in protest against the imprisonment of the Radom workers. Gierek released the Radom workers whose imprisonment had led to the hunger strikes. He held his first ever official conversation with Cardinal Wyszynski on 29 October 1977. It was followed, on 1 December 1977, by an historical meeting between Edward Gierek and Pope Paul VI. Ultimately, Gierek emerged with the claim that no conflict existed in Poland.

The relationship between the government and the Church in Poland improved to some extent. There was a kind of understanding that, if the Church would not actively oppose socialism, the State, in Mary Craig's words, would 'acknowledge its role as a useful moral and educational force in society'. For the time being there was once again a thaw.

Meanwhile, in the implementation of the Council, Wojtyla gave particular emphasis to priestly education. He organized three seminaries in Cracow, in an independent pontifical faculty of theology, which the State tolerated but did not recognize officially. He set up a pastoral Synod for the diocese. He presided over the Octave of Christian prayer for the community, although the scope for ecumenical activity in Poland is limited.

Wojtyla's support and friendship for the university students remained as firm as ever. Mary Craig illustrates this vividly: '"He was in my flat with a group of students once," said a friend, "and I noticed how he listened to each one with enormous concentration and interest. Sometimes he'd say a few words and they'd listen, but they treated him exactly like one of themselves; he was given no more and no less attention than anyone else, though it was obvious they held him in great affection."'

Cardinal Wojtyla did not neglect affairs in Rome. Pope Paul VI invited him to deliver twenty-two meditations for the Holy Father and members of the Curia for the 1976 Lenten retreat. They have since been published under the title *A Sign of Contradiction*, the words being taken from those used by Simeon to Mary at the presentation in the temple. I am sure that I was not alone in selecting the book as my religious reading in Holy Week last year. If one knew nothing else of Cardinal Wojtyla than that he had written this book, one would revere him as a spiritual prophet.

Cardinal Hume has said more than once that the incarnation of Christ lies at the heart of the present Pope's message – that is profoundly true as even the layman can understand. But I suppose that if a distinction can be made, the emphasis in *A Sign of Contradiction* falls on the Cross, which is of course an enrichment of the mystery of the incarnation.

The book begins by quoting the first three chapters of Genesis, which have always had a special significance for the Pope. He finds in them, and in the Creation that they describe, a demonstration of God's love, which should be the starting point of true Christianity. We proceed to the incarnation and to the redemption of fallen man on the Cross. Again quoting his words, 'In the Cross lies the full truth about man, man's true stature, his wretchedness and his grandeur, his worth and the price paid for him.' The present Pope does not shrink from using the word 'mystery' in this and other contexts. 'Redemption,' he writes, 'is the nucleus of the paschal mystery so often remembered by the Second Vatican Council in so many different contexts. In that mystery the Church rediscovered the key to solving, in Christ, all the most difficult problems facing man and the world.' He faces starkly the question of why man had to be redeemed, why he could not redeem himself, and why he needed therefore a divine saviour. 'The mystery,' he says, 'derives from the whole history of man and the world. It springs from the conflict between the word and the anti-word, between love and anti-love.' He admits that 'the mystery implicit in the Cross is far beyond man's intellectual prowess, far beyond human understanding.' We are all, even the Pope himself, groping towards the truth. But no one could read *A Sign of Contradiction* without feeling a little nearer to it.

Cardinal Wojtyla finished his introductory address to the Lenten sermons with this prayer: 'May the "light that shines for the gentiles" be with us in this spiritual undertaking of ours. May this light give us strength and make us capable of accepting and loving the whole

OPPOSITE John Paul II holds a cross during a ceremony during his visit to Poland.

truth of Christ, of loving it all the more, as the world all the more contradicts it.'

Both Cardinal Hume and Archbishop Worlock of Liverpool are friends and admirers of the present Pope. When John Paul was elected Pope, Cardinal Hume spoke as follows: 'I was struck by the impression he gave of strength, determination and durability. Later, I came to appreciate his intellectual ability, his theological grasp and his evident love for his country and his people. He seemed to me to be a hard-headed, but warm-hearted man.' The Cardinal continued: 'As a Pastor working in Poland, he has had to proclaim the Gospel and lead his people in practising Christianity under difficult, and sometimes actively hostile, political conditions. He has shown firm guidance, and yet patience in negotiations. He has maintained and strengthened their faith.'

Archbishop Worlock's praise was just as enthusiastic and based on much more intimate personal knowledge, after working closely with Wojtyla for some thirteen years before his friend was made Pope. He said that he had never known anyone with a finer intellect and he dwelt at length on his strong and attractive character. Wojtyla had an extraordinary capacity to absorb material, to analyse it, to sort it out and then produce a reasoned, often tabulated argument by way of conclusion. He would sit impassively during the discussion, he would wait until nearly the end of the session, when he would raise his hand and deliver a summing-up which won general approval. This task was left to him because his intellectual authority was so accepted, and he was so good at it, that by common consent he was the ideal man. This, too, in spite of the fact that he often took longer than would normally be expected. It was not that he was long-winded, but he liked dealing with a matter thoroughly, and he spoke laboriously, often slowly. However, he was listened to attentively and, where necessary, he was happily allowed to over-run his time.

This deliberateness of thought and speech seems to Archbishop Worlock to be very much part of his total personality. He is always unhurried in thought and action. He has a certain disregard for time, almost a timelessness. He thinks in centuries and refers frequently to the end of this one. No one must expect to hurry him, either in word or deed. In Cardinal Wojtyla's personality, Archbishop Worlock found three qualities which are seldom combined. There was a certain Eastern inscrutability which covered intense concentration; there was great personal warmth in his dealings with individuals, whoever they were. But there was also a certain shyness – the extrovert character of the Pope's tours surprised Worlock. No one who has seen the many photographs of the Pope and Archbishop Worlock together could doubt the warmth; the Eastern inscrutability

OPPOSITE The Pope's personal magnetism is effective whether he is speaking to an individual or a crowd.

The Pope has always had a great love and understanding of children.

could possibly be detected; but the reserve is in no way apparent.

Although Worlock would not describe the Pope as 'conservative', he admits that John Paul 'attaches great importance to tradition and has a tremendous sense of history'. This would fit in with his refusal to be hurried, or to believe that speedy action could be beneficial in the long run. John Paul's own greatest concern, before he became active in the Synods, was with the struggle against atheism. He was, of course, thoroughly well-versed in Marxism through his countless arguments with Marxist intellectuals, old and young, in Poland. In a personal sense, he was tolerant of them. They were all human beings, but the atheism they stood for was ultimately more danger-ous than political Communism.

The sort of topics which have agitated English Catholics in the last thirty years did not come his way until fairly late: birth control, for example, and ecumenism, which could not mean much in Poland, except in connection with Eastern churches. As he began to travel the world in the seventies – though never, as it happens, visiting England – he began to appreciate the concern felt in Western coun-tries about such matters, but they were always secondary in his thoughts. Ecumenically, his main concern was with the Orthodox Churches. A vital interest was the defence of the family.

His theological and philosophical studies had produced in him a reverence for man. Anything that related to the dignity of man excited his extreme interest. It was entirely in character for him to make important contributions to the discussions in Rome about the role of the laity.

It would be wrong to neglect the influence of his Polish background, but just as wrong to neglect his sense of the universal Church. His continuing concern with his homeland and his missionary journeys to all parts of the world underline this double truth.

Although Cardinal Wojtyla made these contributions at the various Synods of the seventies, it appears that he was in no sense a dominant personality during those years. This may have been partly due to the fact that he was very much the number two Polish Cardinal. Until he actually became Pope, he was relatively unobtrusive. When however he was elevated to the Papacy, he expanded naturally in response to the job, drawing easily on his dramatic abilities and experience. A Polish journalist who knew him well, commented on the day of his inauguration as Pope: 'There was a new light in his eyes; he almost seemed to be saying, "Now I am free".'

Chapter 5

A Pilgrim for Christ
1979

JOHN PAUL II made four major tours in 1979, his first year of office. He visited Latin America, Poland, Ireland and the United States, continuing the work Paul VI had started.

What was John Paul's purpose in throwing himself and his message before so many millions of people? Certain aspects of the Pope's personality and teaching have been explained to me authoritatively by Cardinal Hume, although he would not claim a long-standing intimacy with the Pope. Firstly, despite his easy acceptance of contemporary culture, as seen in his way with young people and his mastery of the media, whatever the Pope does or says would be within the age-old tradition of the Catholic Church. Secondly, Pope John Paul II considers that it is his primary duty to preserve 'the deposit of faith'. Thirdly, he strives at all times to supply leadership in the defence of moral ideals.

The Pope sees his role as essentially pastoral or evangelical. It is his overwhelming responsibility to communicate Christian doctrines to the entire world, Catholics and non-Catholics alike. He is a priest; it is his function to hold the host aloft and to carry his saviour everywhere.

He made twenty addresses in Latin America and seventy in Ireland and America, in only eight days. His message is always spiritual rather than political or even social, although his awareness of the appalling poverty of the peoples in the developing countries has lent increasing vehemence to his condemnation of the conditions in which they live. In contrast to these long speeches, his actions were often dramatic and compelling.

There was an interesting background to his visit to Latin America. The meeting of the Bishops at Puebla, Mexico, was to be a follow-up to the great conference at Medellin, opened by Pope Paul VI in 1968. That meeting had indeed been a turning point in the history of the Catholic Church in Latin America. In the famous Medellin manifesto, the Cardinals and Bishops of the South American continent set out to introduce a revolutionary change in the image of the Catholic Church in South America. Hitherto the Church had been

OPPOSITE The Pope visits the Shrine of Our Lady of Guadalupe during his visit to Mexico.

96

identified with the rich and powerful, but now its clergy, high and low, including the nuns and lay activists, were to teach the Gospel by living close to their people.

A new liberation theology emerged. It demanded social improvement in keeping with Christ's teachings in the Gospel. As was pointed out at the time, there was considerable resemblance between some aspects of this teaching and that of the forbidden Marxism.

The programme of liberation theology had been accepted in principle by Pope Paul VI and the majority of the Latin American clergy. Steps were being taken to put it into practice. Not surprisingly, the social improvements met with opposition in conservative quarters; well-to-do Catholics were apprehensive that it would lead to a Socialist or even a Communist takeover, such as that in Cuba under Castro or in Chile under Allende. There was considerable pressure in Rome and in Latin America to dissuade Pope John Paul II from visiting the Puebla Conference. But he seems to have had no hesitation about deciding to make the journey. When he set off from Rome on 25 January 1979, his aeroplane was packed with journalists of every conceivable religious persuasion. Jon Snow of ITN will never forget his first meeting with the Pope. The journalists were astonished when John Paul II left his seat at the front of the aeroplane, and talked to them individually. What struck Jon Snow at once was that the Pope seemed so interested in him, Snow, and no doubt in the other journalists. He discovered rapidly that Jon's father had been

Pope John Paul talking with
enquiring journalists on a
plane journey.

a Bishop. In those few moments of conversation, Jon came to feel that he had known the Pope for many years.

The Pope is frequently described as a fabulous linguist. Jon remembers that when the Pope first talked to him he said, 'I can understand what you say, but my English is rather rusty.' The next time the Pope came round to speak to him, his English had become much more accomplished.

The visit to Latin America constituted Pope John Paul II's first foreign mission since his election. It was felt significant that the trip focused on Mexico; in choosing a Catholic Third World country for his first papal visit, the Pope was possibly reflecting the direction his Papacy might take in years to come. The highlight of this trip was to be the third General Assembly of the Latin American Bishops, held at Puebla, Mexico, on 27 January. The theme of the Assembly was to be evangelization.

Before arriving in Mexico, however, John Paul II chose to break his journey in the Dominican Republic. This visit was interpreted as being symbolic. In stopping here the Pope was following in the footsteps of the first missionaries. The Dominican Republic is part of the island of Hispaniola where the first Mass in the New World was celebrated during Columbus's second expedition in 1493.

The recently elected government declared 25 January a 'Joy Day' in honour of the Pope's arrival: schools, government offices and many private establishments in Santo Domingo, the Republic's capital, closed down for the day to allow people more time to see the Pope during his short visit.

On arriving at Santo Domingo airport, Pope John Paul II knelt and kissed the ground, a custom of Paul VI which the new Pope would follow in all the countries he visited.

He arrived in Mexico City on 27 January. The irreligious President Jose Lopez Portillo gave him a brief formal welcome. Then the Church dignitaries took over. As he drove between Mexico City and Puebla, ten million people lined the route. The speech with which he opened the Conference was long, complicated and ambiguous. He emphasized the Church's involvement with the liberation of 'Man as man', making use of one of his favourite expressions, but he deliberately avoided the term 'liberation theology'. He repudiated the idea that Christ had been a revolutionary, seeking to overthrow a colonial rule. He seemed to be discouraging priests from involvement in political action; clerics were not to be social directors or functionaries of temporal power. Less attention was paid to the later passages of the speech in which he passionately defended the rights attaching to 'Man as man'. The journalists seemed to conclude that he had sided with the conservatives.

OPPOSITE The Pope's welcome in Mexico was tumultuous despite the fact that it is the only Latin American country which has no diplomatic links with the Vatican.

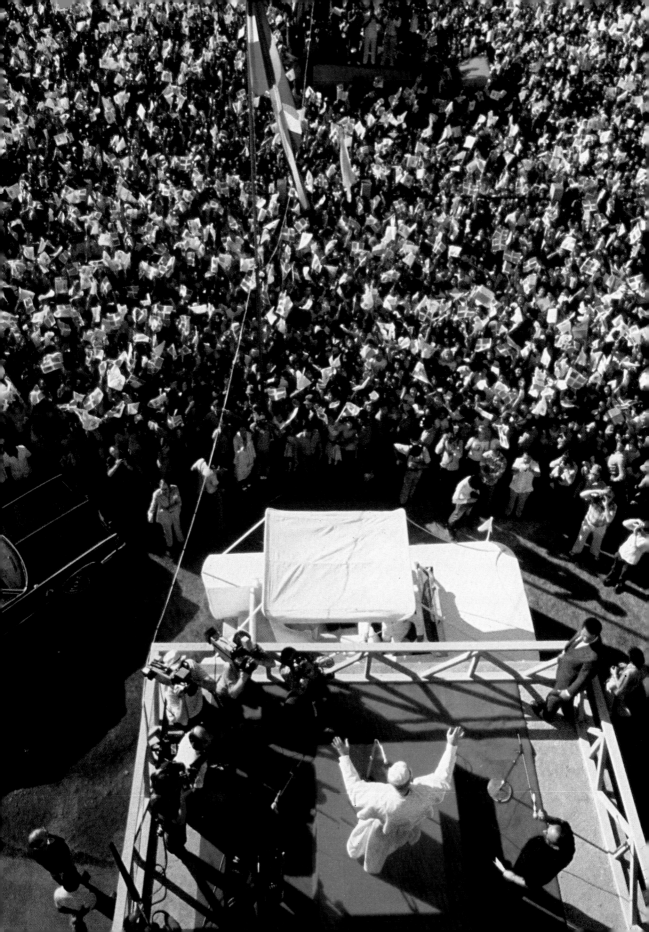

He soon went far to correct that impression. When he addressed 40,000 Indians at Oaxaca he delivered a vehement condemnation of the greed and exploitation that deprived these impoverished people of their right to land and a decent livelihood. Jon Snow, meeting some of the more radical priests two years later, found them satisfied that John Paul II could not have spoken out at that time more strongly than he did against the military dictatorships and the callousness of the rich, and in favour of the poor and needy.

As the Pope's visit proceeded he expressed himself more and more forcibly along these lines. When he returned to Rome he assured 50,000 visitors in St Peter's Square that his journey had been most successful. As always the immediate effect, in terms of political and social change, was arguable. But no one could doubt that the faith of many millions had been strengthened – which, as always, would be John Paul II's prime objective.

The Pope's second foreign tour took him to Poland seven months after his election. For John Paul II it was to be an emotional tour, as he met old friends and revisited places that were so well known to him. The visit started in Warsaw: it took him to Gniezno, the birth-

The Pope, wearing a broad-brimmed sombrero which had been presented to him, endeared himself to the crowds in Oaxaca.

OPPOSITE Vast crowds gathered everywhere in Mexico to meet the Pope and greeted him with cries of 'Viva el Papa!'

place of Polish nationalism; to the hilltop monastery shrine of Czestochowa; to Cracow, the historic city where he had been Archbishop and Cardinal for thirteen years; and to Auschwitz. During the course of his visit he preached thirty sermons covering every aspect of life. Wherever he spoke vast crowds listened, for in Poland Catholicism is synonymous with nationalism: the Pope, in the Poles' eyes, represented both. His reception was, if possible, even more overwhelming than expected.

This nine-day visit to his homeland took place before the far-reaching political events which resulted in the growth of the independent trade union movement and a new sense of self-confidence in Poland. There is no doubt whatever that these striking changes owed much to the visit of the Pope; his gift of inspiring vast crowds of people had never been more in evidence than on his visit to Poland. As one newspaper commented: 'The Pope is a man of rare stature, whose word is more effective than the sword.'

It was the first time that a Roman Catholic Pontiff had visited a Communist-ruled country. The visit was a result of the steady improvement in relations between the Church and the State, but could never have taken place if the Pope himself had not been a Pole. Cardinal Wyszynski had been held in detention for three years in the 1950s. For many years the Communist authorities had refused to allow a visit from a Pope.

As John Paul II arrived in Warsaw, church bells were rung in his honour. He was obviously moved to be back on his native soil, which he characteristically knelt and kissed. He was met by the Communist State authorities and Cardinal Wyszynski. In a statement on his arrival, the Pope expressed 'esteem' for the Communist authorities of his country and said his trip was motivated only by religious considerations.

During the Pope's stay in Warsaw he delivered an address and celebrated an open-air Mass in Victory Square. Here he preached a message of hope and re-birth in Christ. 'Christ,' he said, 'cannot be kept out of the history of man in any part of the globe. The exclusion of Christ from the history of man is an act against man.' The crowd broke into thunderous applause and John Paul II had to wait patiently for silence.

Over two million Poles lined the streets of Warsaw as the Pope passed through the city. It meant that he was constantly behind schedule. The crowds were reluctant to let him move on and John Paul obviously loved to mingle with his fellow countrymen.

As John Paul II proceeded to Gniezno the following day his constant concern for young people was evident. When he offered pontifical High Mass outside the Cathedral he gave an address especially

OPPOSITE The Pope stands dwarfed by the immense concrete cross erected in Warsaw for his visit in 1979.

for the young and spoke with some of them individually. He also led three hours of singing in the evening. The crowds were obviously enraptured, and the Mass lasted for three-and-a-half hours.

The Pope departed from his prepared text as he preached before the Cathedral in Gniezno. He said, 'It would be sad to believe that each Pole and Slav in any part of the world is unable to hear the words of the Pope, this Slav.' He also commented on a banner held in the crowd which read, 'Remember, Father, about your Czech children', saying he was delighted to see it.

The next day saw the Pope at the shrine of Our Lady in the Jasna Gora Monastery in Czestochowa. This shrine has been the home of the famous 'Black Madonna' since 1382. An enormous crowd had assembled in the fields beneath the monastery and the Pope's opening words to the congregation were, 'I am here'. He also broke into song in a rich baritone voice when the crowd started singing.

In addressing Bishops at the Polish Bishops' Conference at Czestochowa John Paul II stressed that 'authentic dialogue between Church and State must respect the convictions of believers, ensure all the rights of the citizens and also the normal conditions for the activity

OPPOSITE Vast crowds converge on the Cathedral at Gniezno, the home of Christianity in Poland.

Pope John Paul II speaking at the monastery of Jasna Gora, Czestochowa.

107

The Pope visiting the monastery of Jasna Gora, Czestochowa, the home of the Black Madonna since 1382.

of the Church as a religious community to which the vast majority of Poles belong.' He spoke strongly of the need for the Church to continue working for freedom of religion.

Before a crowd of 250,000 at a Mass for coal miners from Czestochowa, John Paul II urged Polish workers to resist the atheist propaganda of the nation's Communist rulers. 'Do not,' he warned, 'let yourselves be seduced by the temptation to think that man can fully find himself by denying God, erasing prayer from his life and remaining only a worker.'

It was not until John Paul II arrived in his former diocesan capital of Cracow, however, that the tour reached its emotional climax. Here, the people who had been his diocesan flock before his election awaited his arrival with unrestrained excitement. This was the town where the Pope had secretly studied theology during the war. A crowd of more than one million Poles greeted the Pope when he arrived by helicopter in Cracow. They cheered jubilantly as the Pope said, 'I'm back, my children.'

At Auschwitz, he prayed for the four million people who had died there during World War II, and met former prisoners dressed in the striped uniforms of the death camp. He described the site as 'a place built on hatred and on contempt for man in the name of a crazed ideology'. He also prayed in the cell where Father Maximilian Kolbe was murdered by the Nazis in 1941.

As John Paul II celebrated Mass before a huge crowd crammed

OPPOSITE Pope John Paul II greets miners' sons at Jasna Gora Monastery.

Pope John Paul II, accompanied by Cardinal Wyzsynski, received an enraptured response from the thousands who converged on the monastery of Jasna Gora during his visit to Poland.

OPPOSITE John Paul II on his visit to Auschwitz. He said there, 'It is necessary to think how far hatred could go.'

into the camp he remembered all the nations whose dead were buried there and referred affectionately to the Jews, saying, 'The inscription in Hebrew awakens the memory of the people whose sons and daughters were intended for total extinction. The very people who received from God the commandment "Thou shalt not kill" itself experienced in a special measure what is meant by killing.' Of the inscriptions on the Russian tombs he said, 'I will not add any comment. We all know of what kind of a nation this inscription speaks and we all know what part it played in the last terrible war for the freedom of nations. No nation must ever develop at the expense of another. It must not develop by subordinating another.' Although he was referring to Nazi Germany, there was no doubt in the audience's mind that he was also referring to the fate of contemporary Poland.

The Pope celebrated another Mass at an open-air wooden altar between the railway lines which had brought men from all over Nazi-occupied Europe to be slaughtered in the gas chambers. Here he appealed against any repetition of enslavement, conquest, outrage, exploitation and death. He was speaking, he said, 'not to accuse

but to remind. . . . In the name of all the nations whose rights are being violated and forgotten.'

In contrast to this solemn commemoration to the victims of the holocaust was the simple joy experienced by the Pope on returning to Wadowice, the small town where he was born. Here he was given a rousing welcome by the population of 15,000 swollen by many who had come from neighbouring villages. Here he spoke with his old teacher, Fr Zacher, who is to this day the parish priest of Wadowice.

The high point of the final leg of the Pope's visit came in a meadow outside the centre of Cracow. In this dusty field one-and-a-half million people gathered to hear the Pope's last address in Poland. It was the biggest Mass in history. Many people walked to the site as no transport was provided. In John Paul's address he told the crowd, 'You must be strong, dear brothers and sisters. You must be strong with the strength that comes from faith. . . . Today more than in any other age you need this strength. . . . We must work for peace and reconciliation between the people and the nations of the whole world. We must try to come closer to one another. We must open

OPPOSITE The Pope kneels and prays in Auschwitz in memory of the four million who died there during the Second World War.

A part of the large crowd who came to Auschwitz for a Mass held among the barbed wire and watchtowers of the deathcamp.

Edward Zacher, parish priest
of Wadowice.

the frontiers. . . . So, before I leave you, I wish to give one more look
at Cracow, this Cracow in which every stone and brick is dear to
me. . . . I beg you: never lose your trust, do not be defeated, do not
be discouraged. . . . Never lose your spiritual freedom with which
He makes a human being free.'

Before he left Cracow the Pope again knelt and kissed the ground.
He was obviously moved and tired as he left his native land, wiping
away a tear after his final speech at Cracow airport. On arriving back
in Italy he said, 'I thank God that I was able to see Poland again.'

The visit was a triumph. The general verdict of the Press was:
'John Paul II is the greatest communicator of our time. It was a
superb religious manifestation, of unforeseeable secular significance.'
In the words of the *Catholic Herald*: 'In nine emotion-packed days,
the Pope had brought new hope to his defiant Catholic countrymen'.

In September, John Paul II left Rome once again, this time to visit Ireland. For me, inevitably, the Pope's visit to Ireland occupies a place apart. I was at Phoenix Park, Dublin, and Knock in the west of Ireland, and shared to the full a never-to-be-forgotten experience with the vast crowds who flocked to greet the Pope. It was a profoundly Catholic moment but one in which non-Catholics participated joyfully. There can be arguments about the after-effects of his visit. There can be no argument about the mutual love that flowed between him and his audience. The three-and-a-half million people who make up Catholic Ireland from the north and the south seemed to be pouring out their very soul.

The world outside, including Britain, were inclined to concentrate on the political implications of the visit, for Lord Mountbatten and others with him had been brutally murdered not long before.

Wherever he went on his tours, John Paul II made a point of speaking to the ordinary people.

When John Paul II arrived in Ireland, Cardinal O'Fiaich greeted him with the words, 'He comes, a messenger of peace to a troubled land.'

When it was prudently decided that it was unwise for him to visit Northern Ireland, attention centred on the lengths he would go to in denouncing violence.

In the event he spoke on matters such as these with a firmness that appeared to satisfy the British government and at the same time convince patriotic Irishmen that he fully understood the underlying causes of the horrifying violence. During World War II someone once congratulated Mr Churchill on a magnificent speech he had just delivered. He replied, 'If it was only a question of making speeches, I would have beaten Hitler long ago.' If the Pope's words and his all-embracing personality could have had their due reward, the gunmen of Ireland would have thrown away their weapons then and there.

'I have heard,' John Paul told his audience, 'the voice of the Irish calling me, and so I have come to you, to all of you in Ireland.' His hour-long homily at Drogheda in Cardinal O'Fiaich's diocese of Armagh, twenty-five miles from the Ulster border, aroused most attention. It was attended by many thousands from Northern and Southern Ireland. They heard the Pope condemn violence deliberately and repeatedly, while not overlooking the claims of justice. 'The tragic events taking place in Northern Ireland do not have their

source in the fact of belonging to different Churches and con-
fessions. . . . This is not – despite what is so often repeated before
world opinion – a religious war, a struggle between Catholics and
Protestants. On the contrary, Catholics and Protestants, as people
who confess Christ . . . are seeking to draw closer to one another in
unity and peace.'

The eyes and the minds of the enormous crowd were fixed on
John Paul as he stood before them. 'Christianity does not command
us to close our eyes to difficult human problems. . . . What Christianity does forbid is to seek solutions to these situations by ways of
hatred, by the murdering of defenceless people, by the methods of
terrorism.' He made a passionate plea for peace: 'To all of you who
are listening I say: do not believe in violence; do not support
violence. It is not the Christian way. . . . I appeal to you, in language
of passionate pleading. On my knees I beg you to turn away from
the paths of violence and to return to the ways of peace. You may

The crowds in Phoenix Park,
Dublin, were so great that
they seemed to include most
of the population of the
country.

Pope John Paul II celebrates
Mass in Phoenix Park,
Dublin.

claim to seek justice. . . . But violence destroys the work of justice.
Further violence in Ireland will only drag down to ruin the land you
claim to love and the values you claim to cherish.'

The Pope then spoke directly to young people, who are perhaps
most vulnerable to the attractions of violence as a means of seeking
justice: 'I appeal to young people who may have become caught up
in organizations engaged in violence. I say to you, with all the love
I have for you, with all the trust I have in young people: do not
listen to voices which speak the language of hatred, revenge, retali-
ation. Do not follow any leaders who train you in the ways of
inflicting death. Love life, respect life. . . . My dear young people, if
you have been caught up in the ways of violence . . . come back to
Christ, whose parting gift to the world was peace.'

John Paul II did not lay the blame for the continued violence at the
door of young people alone: 'And to you, Fathers and Mothers, I
say: teach your children how to forgive, make your homes places of
love and forgiveness; make your streets and neighbourhoods centres
of peace and reconciliation. It would be a crime against youth and
their future to let even one child grow up with nothing but the
experience of violence and hate.'

His appeal for justice and peace rang out over the heads of the

thousands gathered before him: 'Peace cannot be established by violence. . . . It is Jesus himself who said: "All who take the sword will perish by the sword". . . . I pray with you that the moral sense and Christian conviction of Irish men and women may never become obscured and blunted by the lie of violence, that nobody may ever call murder by any other name. . . .'

Priests waiting to distribute Holy Communion in Phoenix Park, Dublin.

Towards the end of his speech, he reached out to Irish Protestants, offering them his love and trust: 'To Catholics, to Protestants, my message is peace and love. May no Irish Protestant think that the Pope is an enemy, a danger or a threat. My desire is that instead Protestants would see in me a friend and a brother in Christ. . . . Let history record that, at a difficult moment in the experience of the people of Ireland, the Bishop of Rome set foot in your land, that he was with you and prayed with you for peace and reconciliation, for the victory of justice and love over hatred and violence.'

This speech, so carefully devised yet so obviously heartfelt, was delivered to a crowd who stood in absolute silence, only punctuating the speech with applause every time that John Paul condemned violence. The speech was praised by most politicians in Northern Ireland and Dublin, although the Reverend Ian Paisley and Enoch Powell thought it comforted the IRA.

The Pope at the shrine of the
Virgin Mary at Knock on
the west coast of Ireland.

The celebrations at Knock provided a special reason for the whole visit to Ireland. The centenary of the 'Sanctuary of the Mother of God' at Knock constituted a 'providential' occasion, as John Paul put it, for the visit. He began his sermon at Knock with the words: 'Here I am at the goal of my journey to Ireland.'

The fame of Knock dates from 21 August 1879, when twenty-two villagers saw three illuminated figures whom they took to be Mary, Joseph and John the Evangelist against the south gable wall of Knock church. But it took fifty years for the claims to be officially recognized. From 1929 onwards pilgrimages to Knock became frequent. From 1954, after the Assumption to heaven of the Blessed Virgin Mary had become an official Dogma of the Church, Rome indicated an increasing degree of recognition: Pope Pius XII blessed a Knock banner; John XXIII presented the Shrine with a candle; and Paul VI allowed pilgrims there to have Communion twice in the day. By 1979 Cardinal O'Fiaich was claiming in effect that the Virgin Mary had indeed revealed herself there and the visit of the Pope was widely regarded as an ultimate confirmation.

In the morning, the whole world seemed to be converging on

Knock; many covered the last few miles on foot. The event fulfilled all expectations, although the Pope, taking infinite trouble over every human being he meets, is inclined to fall behind schedule. The most moving moment of the visit came when the Pope, mitred and wearing white vestments, knelt to pray at the gable of the old church where the silent apparition had taken place. He remained there for some minutes, eyes closed, head bowed in prayer.

'The Pope loves children,' the women in the crowd said to one another at Knock as John Paul II slowly and deliberately bent over the smallest persons presented to him. But for me perhaps the most poignant moment was his visit to the Basilica and the 3,000 disabled who awaited him there. He showed the same deliberateness as he had to the children and, if possible, an even greater tenderness as he passed from one wheelchair to another. His short address was just about perfect: 'Today I am happy to be with the sick and the handicapped. I have come to give witness to Christ's love for you, and to tell you that the Church and the Pope love you too. They reverence and esteem you. They are convinced that there is something very special about your mission in the Church.' It takes a mental talent of a high order to think of such words; spiritual genius to mean them heart and soul.

No one could improve on John Whale's description in *The Pope from Poland* of Pope John Paul's address at the Galway Mass for young people before yet another vast audience. Whale argues that outside Poland Pope John Paul II, in spite of his amazing linguistic gifts, is at his best as a communicator without words. He goes on:

Invalids wait to be blessed by the Pope at the Basilica at Knock.

'Pursing his lips to retain his self-control as he looked out over a sea of cheering devotees; listening rapt to a choir singing, the crucifix in his crozier held against his cheek; hugging a boy blinded by a rubber bullet in an encounter with the British Army in Derry – in much that he did he showed beyond argument, whatever the counter-implications of his sterner sayings, that his interest in human lives was universal; and it was universal because it started from the particular.'

Whale refers to John Paul II's 'sterner sayings'. Certainly he did not mince his words before his young audience: 'Yes, dear young people, do not close your eyes to the moral sickness that stalks your society today, and from which your youth alone will not protect you. How many young people have already warped their consciences and have substituted the true joy of life with drugs, sex, alcohol, vandalism and empty pursuit of mere material possessions.' And there was a good deal more to the same effect. But when he reached his conclusion and his simple words rang out: 'Young people of Ireland, I love you,' the tide of approval was overwhelming. The cheering and singing went on for fourteen minutes. His claim that 'I know young people' was vindicated for all time in Ireland.

Galway Racecourse where the Pope met thousands of young Irish people. Both they and the Pope seemed to thoroughly enjoy the meeting.

Those who were looking for some new expression of opinion about the situation in Northern Ireland in every speech he gave may have been disappointed by John Paul II's address at Phoenix Park although it was known at the time that he would be speaking at Drogheda that afternoon. For me, just one of the thousands standing in the crowd, it expressed his spiritual priorities more clearly and decisively than any of the other speeches. It was a sermon and not one readily summarized. Later, there was a good deal of comment, not all of it favourable, on his attack on 'consumerism' in a country which, until recently, had so little to consume. But as I interpreted and still interpret the address, his message was more deep-rooted. He was, above all, concerned to proclaim the age-old connection between the deepest Irish feelings and the Eucharist. From the beginning of his speech, he drove that point home again and again: 'As I stand at this moment, a pilgrim for Christ to the land from which so many pilgrims for Christ, *peregrini pro Christo*, went out over Europe, the Americas, Australia, Africa, Asia, I am living a moment of intense emotion. As I stand here, in the company of so many hundreds of thousands of Irish men and women, I am thinking of how many times, across how many centuries, the Eucharist has been celebrated in this land.

'. . . From the Upper Room in Jerusalem, from the Last Supper, in a certain sense, the Eucharist writes the history of human hearts and of human communities. Let us reflect on all those who, being nourished on the Body and Blood of the Lord, have lived and died on this island, bearing in themselves, because of the Eucharist, the pledge of eternal life. . . .'

On leaving Ireland, the Pope referred to the Irish devotion to the Mass, saying, 'For them, a whole Catholic people is seen to be faithful to the Lord's command, "Do this in memory of me".'

The Pope followed this with his attack on materialism and con-sumerism and the so-called freedom arising from it which is in reality a new form of slavery. Then he moved on to his triumphant conclusion: '. . . Thus I can proclaim the vivifying reality of con-version through the Eucharist and the Sacrament of Penance in the midst of the present generation of the sons and daughters of Ireland. METANOEITE, "Be converted!"'

Flying from Ireland to America, John Paul II arrived at Logan International Airport, Boston, punctual for the first and last time dur-ing his visit. He was greeted by a crowd of two million. This was a pattern that would be followed in the other American cities he visited. 'From the moment,' to quote Fr Francis Murphy, Rector of the Holy Redeemer College in Washington, 'he kissed the ground on his arrival in Boston, the Polish Pope had simply mesmerized the American public, occupying the major portion of the television and radio broadcasts, taking over the youth, and receiving the homage of politicians, academics, clergy and businessmen, as well as the poor in the slum areas of Harlem and the Bronx.' He became the first Pope ever to set foot inside the White House, to be received with the greatest warmth and goodwill. President Carter hailed him as a pilgrim of peace. On the second day in New York, the Pope attended a morning service at St Patrick's Cathedral. Later he met a group of 20,000 children in Madison Square Gardens and accepted gifts from them which included a pair of jeans and a guitar. 60,000 people

OPPOSITE The Pope receives the traditional tickertape welcome in New York.

John Paul II is received by the then President of the United States, Jimmy Carter and his wife Rosalyn in the White House.

John Paul II before the
United Nations' Assembly
where he emphatically
denounced the worldwide
violation of human rights.

packed Shea Stadium for his final New York appearance. Undaunted
by the bad weather, they listened attentively to his words of fare-
well to them.

The address John Paul II delivered to the General Assembly of
the United Nations in New York is described by Fr Murphy as a
masterpiece of forensic oratory. He began with an eloquent tribute
to the United Nations itself: 'It will never cease to be the forum, the
high tribune from which all man's problems are appraised in truth
and justice.' He described the Universal Declaration of Human
Rights, 1948, as 'a milestone on the long and difficult path of the
human race'. John Paul II returned again and again to the subject of
human rights. His other main themes were the pre-eminence of
spiritual as compared with material values; the need for a far more
just distribution of material goods both within individual societies
and on the planet as a whole; and the need, spoken with passionate
urgency, to arrest the Arms race before the whole world was destroyed by it. If it could hardly be claimed that anything he said was
totally new, there can have been no more complete or powerful
diagnosis of the present world situation delivered in our time. John

Paul II left no doubt in the minds of the secular audience about the direction in which an ultimate solution must lie.

From New York he moved on to Philadelphia, where he won the hearts of thousands of Spanish and Ukranian immigrants by preaching to them in their native tongue. He praised American principles of freedom but said that this freedom must be tempered by 'the knowledge of truth as taught by the Catholic Church'. He stressed that, 'In today's society we see so many disturbing tendencies and so much laxity regarding the Christian view of sexuality that have all one thing in common: recourse to the concept of freedom to justify any behaviour that is no longer consonant with the true moral order and the teaching of the Church.' He spoke out for restraint in a society where the individual is presented with a vast range of choices, and he warned against the permissiveness and moral corruption which can result from Western civilization.

In Chicago, the traditional home of Poles in America, with a huge Catholic population, it is not surprising that his reception was ecstatic, almost delirious. In the course of this visit to Chicago he made his most unequivocal statement of the Church's attitude to artificial birth control and divorce. He made no concession to either. He said with emphasis, 'I myself today with the same conviction as Paul VI ratify the teaching which was put forth by my predecessor.'

One event aroused considerable public interest when he was addressing 5,000 nuns at the national Shrine of the Immaculate Conception in Washington. One of them stepped forward from the

The Pope waves to 750,000 people in New York's Yankee Stadium where he was given a reception worthy of a superstar.

127

The Pope visited the huge Catholic population of Chicago. Chicago is the home of more Poles than any city apart from Warsaw.

assembled group. The nun, Sister Teresa Kane, kneeling before the Pontiff, urged him to 'be open to, and to respond to, the voices coming from the women of this country whose desire is for serving in and through the Church as fully participating members. I urge you to be mindful of the intense suffering and pain which is part of the life of many women in these United States.' However, in what was described in the *Daily Telegraph* in October 1979 as 'a rebuff for nun over women priests' plea', John Paul II stuck rigidly later to his declaration that the Roman Catholic Church cannot, and will not, ordain women. He also reminded the nuns that no woman, not even Mary, had been present at the Last Supper: the role of women in the Church was steeped in tradition. Although many of the nuns must have been disappointed with the Pope's written reply, it did not prevent them giving him a warm ovation at the end of his address.

The high point of John Paul II's stay in Washington came when he celebrated Mass for nearly a million people on Washington Mall. Many had camped overnight on this strip of parkland. Many more flocked there in the morning. This was the final Mass he celebrated in America and it lasted nearly two hours.

The Pope had been thunderously applauded by almost every crowd he had addressed during his stay in America. The warmth with which he was received surprised many people for, as the *Daily Telegraph* reported, 'Neither the Pope nor those closest to him had dreamed that he would receive the kind of adoration bestowed on

OPPOSITE At the invitation of one of the parishioners of the town, the Pope visited the rural community of Des Moines, Iowa.

129

At the end of his American trip, John Paul II visited Washington where he delivered a resounding condemnation of consumerism.

him by Americans of so many diverse religions and philosophies.' Yet it was also felt, as the *Observer* reported on 7 October 1979, 'the hysteria with which he [the Pope] has been received . . . has tended to obscure the true nature of his messages.' The Pope, it was said by some, had 'chastened and admonished' much more than he had offered 'thanks of praise'. Again some wondered if the Pope's strictly 'conservative' views were the right ones for present-day society. However, few failed to respond to his impassioned pleas for economic and social justice, for human rights and for an end to violence.

When the Pope finally returned to Rome after the Irish and American visits, he had travelled ten thousand miles in nine days, seen ten million people, slept an average of four-and-a-half hours per night and delivered seventy-two discourses. If his prepared addresses had been deeply impressive, the impromptu ones were hardly less so. When one of the vast crowds roared at him, 'Pope John Paul II, we want you,' he immediately replied, as always with the perfect timing of a fine actor, 'Pope John Paul II, I want *you*.'

John Paul II finished his travels with a carefully considered visit to Turkey. On the face of things, the purpose of his journey to this Muslim country was to participate in the feast of St Andrew with the Greek Orthodox Patriarch Demetrius I. A symbolic ecumenical significance was provided by the fact that St Andrew had been the brother of St Peter. For the first time in over a thousand years, the Pope and Patriarch attended each other's liturgies. They did not participate in the Eucharist together. It was thought that some of the fourteen independent Orthodox leaders, Russian, Bulgarian, Coptic, Rumanian and so on, might have considered such an action to be premature and offensive.

John Paul II arrived in Istanbul without fanfare and spent the afternoon with the civil authorities. He spent his first night in the home of the apostolic delegate where Pope John XXIII had resided as the papal representative of Greece and Turkey throughout World War II. On the following day he visited the shrine of the Blessed Virgin at Ephesus.

The Pope's visit to Turkey was a 'low profile' operation intended

The Pope speaks with the Greek Orthodox Patriarch Demetrius I while on a stop-over visit to Turkey.

to support the political position of the Orthodox Patriarch, and to represent a few cautious steps in an ecumenical direction.

During the year, John Paul II published three documents of considerable, if varying, importance. On 1 January 1979 he delivered a message for World Peace Day. On the face of it, he was saying a number of worthy things which had been said often enough before by religious and other leaders. Yet there are ways of speaking about peace which touch the heart, because of the strength and coherence of the total message. Perhaps the most striking passages on this occasion were those which condemned the Arms race. He would be returning often to this theme, making no concession to those in the West who are convinced that all blame lies with the other side.

His first encyclical, *Redemptor Hominis*, was published on 4 March. Cardinal Hume has told me that he regards this encyclical as a guide :o spiritual meditation.

No document of this kind can readily be subjected to a quasi-political test. Nevertheless it does have practical implications. John Paul II presents ecumenism as a central dimension of the Church's mission. He points the way to dialogue with the other great world religions, which possess 'treasures of human spirituality and enshrine implicitly "seeds of the Gospel".' He has vital things to say about the alienation of modern man, traced by Marx to capitalism, but much closer in the mind of John Paul II to the biblical idea of sin. In the course of the encyclical, he once again asserts the fundamental and inalienable human right to freedom of religion, which he had already championed in the Council long before. The curtailment and violation of religious freedom are 'in contrast with Man's dignity and his objective rights'. Those who hoped that the Pope would come down on the 'right' or the 'left' side in a quasi-political sense must have been disappointed. He was not thinking in those terms; it was not that kind of discourse.

The third document, *Letter to Priests*, has not the same status as the encyclical. It has been described by Peter Hebblethwaite as 'uncompromisingly conservative'. Yet Hebblethwaite admits that it is a moving letter in which the Pope tries to place himself on the same level as his fellow priests. It seemed to inaugurate a tougher line in granting dispensations to priests who wished to surrender their orders while remaining in the Church. But an attitude of this kind had already been initiated by Pope Paul VI at the end of his life and was part of the developing consensus at the time of his election. The Pope wrote unequivocally in the *Letter to Priests*: 'It is a matter here of keeping one's word to Christ and the Church.' He felt poignantly that his beloved priesthood was being undermined by the large numbers of priests who were finding it not too difficult to obtain

OPPOSITE Pope John Paul II about to bless a crowd during his visit to America.

The Pope delivered a controversial reiteration of traditional Catholic values to the American Bishops in Chicago.

permission to abandon their vocation and embrace a secular life.

The year ended with a controversial event. In December a Belgian Dominican, Eduard Schillebeeckx, came under criticism from the Congregation for the Doctrine of Faith, formally known as the Holy Office. The Congregation is one of the most influential departments in the Curia. It had been 'reformed' by Pope Paul VI but now seemed to be adopting a tougher line which, inevitably, was attributed to the influence of Pope John Paul II. Schillebeeckx was summoned to Rome for discussions on the radical views in his bestselling book *Jesus: an experiment in christology*. This was not to be an isolated case. On 15 December the day Schillebeeckx's interrogation was concluded, the Congregation for the Doctrine of Faith produced a declaration which said 'Professor Hans Küng could no longer be regarded as a Catholic theologian.' He had questioned, for example, papal infallibility. His mandate to teach as a Catholic theologian was withdrawn. Four days later the German Bishops published further details but added that Küng remained a priest and a Catholic.

A loud outcry arose in predictable quarters, both Catholic and non-Catholic. I personally cannot for a moment accept the idea that it was obviously wrong and unfair and illiberal to deprive Dr Küng of his official status. No one supposed that it would interfere with his livelihood. Surely these questions ought to be asked, in regard to a Church which is supposed to stand for a consistent body of doctrine. Are there any limits to what a Catholic should be allowed to say on doctrinal matters, without being pronounced a heretic? Are there any narrower limits to what a priest should be permitted to say? Are there any still narrower limits to what anyone who is an official theologian should be allowed to say? The answer to all three questions is surely 'yes'.

Personally I was not in the least surprised that such a fate should have befallen Dr Küng. I have met him twice and found him charming and modest; he has certainly a brilliant intellect. I have read and enjoyed and benefited from several of his books, including his mighty work *On Being a Christian*. But it has never occurred to me that his views were in any sense the official views of the Catholic Church. It seems just as well that the point has been clarified.

In political life, we are not unfamiliar with this kind of situation. When Clement Attlee (later Lord Attlee) became Prime Minister in 1945, Professor Harold Laski, that year Chairman of the Labour Party, insisted on offering him unsolicited guidance. Attlee finally retorted: 'A period of silence on your part would be welcome.' It would be understandable if the Pope felt the same about Dr Küng, though he would never have expressed himself as abruptly as Lord Attlee.

The Pope on 22 May 1980 commended the German Bishops for their collaboration with the Congregation for the Doctrine of Faith. He called it an example of collegiality. Küng had expressed reservations concerning infallibility. 'Infallibility,' said the Pope, 'was a gift of Christ to the Church. . . . When this essential basis of faith is weakened and destroyed, the most elementary truths of our faith begin to collapse.'

Taken all in all, 1979 had been as remarkable a year as any in the recorded life of a Papacy.

Chapter 6

Wider still and wider
1980

N O BISHOP ever took his diocesan duties more seriously than
Wojtyla did when he was Bishop, Archbishop and Cardinal
of Cracow from 1958 to 1978. He has been just as anxious to
be a real Bishop of Rome of a kind not known for centuries.

Pastoral work in Rome, it is admitted on all sides, had long been
neglected. The Popes were sovereigns of the papal states until they
were deprived of their temporal power in 1870. But Popes continued to live in the Vatican; they did not recognize the new Italian
State. The quarrel between the Papacy and the State was resolved on
paper by the Lateran Treaty signed with Mussolini in 1929, but still
the Popes rarely left the Vatican. Paul VI was seriously concerned
about the problems of the City but emerged only occasionally from
the Vatican to visit his diocese. The clergy of Rome would go to see
him, but the meetings were formal occasions.

John Paul II has adopted a totally different approach. Each weekend when he is in Rome, John Paul devotes most of Sunday to a
pastoral visit to a Roman parish. In preparation for this he meets
with the parish priest and the Cardinal Vicar of Rome. Roman
parishes have never seen so much of the Pope. His visit to the Lateran
Palace on 21 February 1980 was regarded as highly significant. The
Church of St John Lateran is the Pope's cathedral church and Popes
had lived in the Lateran Palace until 1347. The three-hour meeting
with the Pope is remembered by the participants as an inspiring
occasion. Pope John Paul admitted his ignorance of the diocese and
promised to try and put that right.

Pope John Paul has not only visited the parish churches in Rome
but also the hospitals, the hostels for drug addicts, and the prisons
for young offenders. He knows only too well the gravity of the social
and religious issues prevalent in his diocese. It was said that, as the
gloomy statistics were recited to the Pope as he travelled around
Rome, his optimism was less noticeable than usual. His determination to improve matters is inflexible.

John Paul II has also travelled more widely in Italy than his pre-
decessors. John XXIII had made a mild break with tradition. He

OPPOSITE The Pope as
Pastor of Rome visits the
victims of the earthquake
which devastated the town
of Irpina and made thousands
homeless.

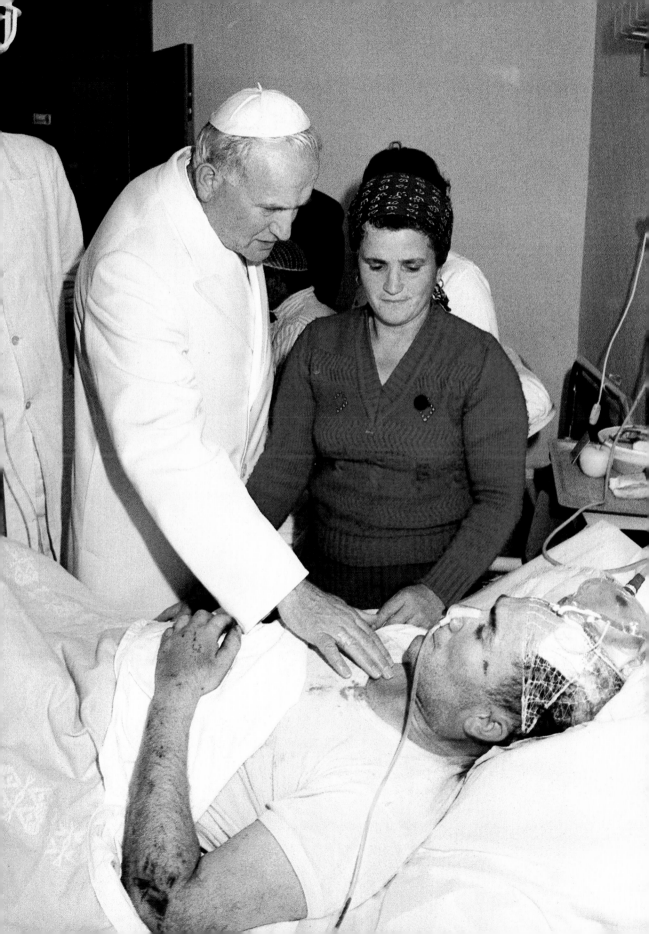

The visit of the Pope to the steelworks at Terni

went by train to Assisi and Loretto, but he still had to emphasize that he was not reviving claims to the former papal states. The situation has been somewhat easier for a non-Italian Pope. He has not had, or attempted to have, the kind of contact with the leading Christian Democrats enjoyed by both John XXIII and Paul VI. He has struck up an excellent relationship with the Socialist President. He has referred to Italy as 'my second homeland' and he speaks the language well.

His first two major expeditions in Italy were to Naples and Turin. He began his visit to Naples on 21 October 1979 at the Marian Shrine of Pompeii. He used words about his spectacular visits that countered objections. He said that the essence of his ministry was 'to open the way of the Holy Spirit'. All the rest, he said, 'is a display that, humanly speaking, could be considered superficial.'

A Lord Chancellor of brilliant forensic gifts once told me that the secret of advocacy was to find out the worst your opponent could say about you, and then say it yourself. The Pope has not often

The Pope among pilgrims in
St Peter's Square

needed to follow that advice, but at Naples he seems to have adopted
it to general satisfaction. The charge of play-acting, levelled at this
admittedly great actor, was effectively rebutted. Naples, for all its
poverty, was in festive mood as it awaited the arrival of John Paul,
the first Pope to visit the city since 1870, and he responded magni-
ficently. Enzo Mangia writing in *L'Osservatore Romano* commented
emotionally that 'the Neopolitans saw in the Vicar of Christ their
Sun, the light that recreates inner order. . . . Thus the profane was
transformed into the sacred, reversing the secularizing trends of the
age.' A sophisticated critic commented: 'Forsooth! That is the kind
of thing that gives the Vatican newspaper a bad name.' But sophisti-
cation is not necessarily the proper state of mind in which to appreciate this kind of celebration. The Pope's sentiments were impeccably
humanitarian: 'Charity, the first duty of every Christian, does not
make justice superfluous; and justice, the cardinal virtue, calls for
and is filled up by charity.' Everyone could indeed applaud, including
the many Communists in the audience.

139

Turin was undergoing a recession in the Fiat car industry when the Pope visited it on 13 April 1980. It is also a centre of terrorist organizations. The Pope criticized capitalism and Communism equally sharply: 'There is on the one hand the rationalist, scientific, Enlightenment approach of the secular so-called "Liberalism" of Western nations, which carries with it the radical denial of Christianity; and on the other hand, the ideology and praxis of atheistic "Marxism" whose materialistic principles are taken to their most extreme consequences in various forms of contemporary terrorism.' It is apparent that the Pope's even-handed condemnation, both of capitalism and Communism, is not some clever diplomatic ploy; it springs from the depths of his conviction.

In March he went to Norcia where St Benedict was born. He dwelt on the theme of St Benedict as a peace-maker and architect of civilization. He also discussed the Benedictine motto: *Laborare est orare* (To work is to pray). It is, incidentally, my own family motto. Not all his visits were formal occasions. For instance, he went to see victims of an earthquake in their new pre-fabricated homes.

The Pope paid a visit to the ancient city of Siena, home of St Catherine, the patroness of Italy, on 14 September 1980.

OPPOSITE The Pope speaking to the people of the devastated earthquake region.

141

In early autumn John Paul II visited Aquila, Siena and Otranto. The visit to Siena has been described as the most controversial of his Italian journeys. He went to celebrate the six-hundredth anniversary of the death of St Catherine who, with St Francis, is the patron saint of Italy. He took the opportunity to deliver what was understood to be a vehement anti-abortion statement. 'The Church judges no one,' he cried, 'but it cannot fail to bear witness to the truth. Every attack on the child in its mother's womb is a great blow to conscience. It is a great sorrow.' The crowd of 40,000 roared their applause. Certainly, the issue of abortion in Italy is as controversial as any issue could be. It was legalized in 1978. In 1980 the Radical Party were attempting to liberalize the law on abortion still further by means of a referendum. The Pro-Life Movement hit back with a demand for a referendum of their own. The Radical and Socialist parties saw the Pope's intervention as flagrant interference in the internal affairs of the Republic of Italy. The Socialist leader, Bertino Craci, said in the Italian parliament that John Paul II was a foreigner who did not understand the Italian constitution. The Bishops replied furiously that the Pope had a perfect right and duty to proclaim moral principles whenever and wherever he spoke. Pope John Paul II obviously had no intention of being closely linked with any political party, but he had just as little intention of being muzzled: he will speak as freely in Italy as he has done in Poland and communicate directly with the mass of the people.

There is, admittedly, an underlying dilemma here which confronts all religious leaders, exalted or humble. Are they to confine themselves to statements of principles so innocuous that political leaders of all kinds can pay lip-service to them? Or are they to point to practical implications which may delight some and infuriate others?

1980 saw the amazing tempo of work and travel maintained. Apart from his pastoral work as Bishop of Rome, John Paul II regularly produces two or three speeches a day. He is sent countless letters, telegrams and messages and receives a constant stream of visitors. He presides over the Church and the task of guiding its vast bureaucracy. In 1980 he promoted and played a leading part in two highly significant Synods. He also undertook two major tours to Africa and Brazil, a long weekend visit to Paris and a brief journey to West Germany in November.

Even with his great sources of energy, the Pope is only able to fit everything in by sticking to a set pattern of life. Especially favoured friends are invited to Mass at 7 a.m. Afterwards they usually stay to talk over breakfast. The stream of visitors goes on and on throughout the day. But there are numerous official meetings with a

formal exchange of speeches: ambassadors flow in to present their credentials; President Jimmy Carter 'dropped in by helicopter' on 21 June on his way to a summit meeting; Queen Elizabeth II, as will be described later, was received on 17 October. Sometimes these visits involve negotiations; sometimes nothing more than courtesy, though it is not easy to draw the line.

The renowned 'General Audiences' take place on Wednesdays, in St Peter's Square from spring to autumn, and indoors during the winter months. These General Audiences as developed by John Paul though not originated by him are described by Hebblethwaite as 'part religious rally, part lecture, part prayer and part entertainment'. The Pope moves through the aisles in his white-painted jeep in St Peter's Square for about half an hour. In Italian, he reads out his pre-pared speech which, in 1980, was an exposition of the opening chapters of the book of Genesis. He reads a summary of what he has said in the languages spoken by the various groups present. He gives the blessing, and finishes with some informal words. There will always be a special word for the sick and the newly wed. After that, he leads the singing of the 'Our Father', and then the various

Large crowds attend a General Audience in St Peter's Square.

143

groups may themselves provide entertainment. Some of the Audiences have lasted over three hours. At noon on Sunday morning he delivers a ten-minute homily from a window and then meets the crowd and speaks more informally.

John Paul has frequently said Mass in St Peter's Square apart from on the traditional occasions of Christmas and Easter. I can speak at first hand of what this can mean to an individual pilgrim. My elder sister, in her late seventies, sold her house in London and made her home in Rome, being received into the Catholic Church in St Peter's. She might not agree that she had gone there simply to be near the Pope. She finds Rome itself the centre of the world. But she did not decide to alter her whole way of life until after John Paul had become Pope, and the Audiences just described have made her feel very close to him, although she has not met him in person. Those who draw similar inspiration from him are, no doubt, 'like the sand in the sea innumerable'.

The Roman Curia is the Pope's bureaucratic instrument; Englishmen who have many dealings with the Vatican describe the administration generally as something between Whitehall and the Court. If the Roman Curia can sometimes be said to have had a mind of its own, the same remark has been made just as often about the British Civil Service, though they also are supposed to be 'obedient servants'.

The Secretariat of State is now recognized as the Curia's main executive and co-ordinating body. The majority of its members are Italian. In the estimation of Peter Nichols, doyen of Rome correspondents, the three men who count most in the Church's central administrative life are the Cardinal-Secretary of State, the Substitute and the Secretary of the Council for Public Affairs. The historic form of the Curia emerges little changed from what it was in the sixteenth century. New offices have been added and sixteen new bodies have been created as the result of the Council. The officials in these offices show a more international character. There are almost as many non-Italians as there are Italians. But the Secretariat for Christian Unity, established by Pope John in 1960, alone seems to carry much weight.

The Synod of Bishops was established by Pope Paul VI in September 1965. It was not to be part of the Curia and it came directly under the Pope's authority. It is consultative and, therefore, cannot force any policy on a Pontiff. It meets every three years apart from special meetings. Although there is no question of this at the present time, it is possible that the Synod of Bishops could become the germ of a legislative organ which the Curia would bow to.

The Pope's first trip in 1980 was to Africa. Pope Paul VI had paid it a flying visit. Pope John Paul II stayed there for ten days. He delivered just over seventy sermons and addresses and visited six

countries: Zaire, the People's Republic of the Congo, Kenya, Upper
Volta, Ghana and the Ivory Coast – an ambitious and exhausting
journey. Five of the ten days were spent in Zaire, which has the
largest population, twenty-two million, half of which is Catholic. In
his key speech to the Bishops the Pope stressed the limits of Africanization. It is hotly debated how far the Church in Africa should be
adapted to local cultures. Pope John Paul laid down that the liturgy
should maintain a substantial unity with the Roman rites: 'Any
innovations should be approved and "dignified".' In an address to
young couples he used Genesis to demonstrate that monogamous
marriage as a lifelong and equal partnership comes to us from God.

He was not prepared to repeat what Paul VI had said in Kampala:
'You can and must have an African Christianity.' He recognized,
however, that African cultural elements, suitably 'refined and purified', could be introduced into Christianity. Missionaries must begin
by building on the 'values of African society'. These he described
in noble language in his speech to the President of Ghana on 8 May.
He stressed the diversity of Africa, but a diversity bound together by
the unity of its culture. He referred to a 'vision of the world where

The colourful reception for
the Pope on his arrival in
Zaire

the sacred is central; a deep awareness of the link between Creator
and nature; a great respect for all life; a sense of family and of community that blossoms into an open and joyous hospitality; reverence
for dialogue as a means of settling differences; spontaneity and the
joy of living expressed in poetic language, song and dance.' He insisted that 'the African soul was naturally religious if not naturally
Christian'.

In Kinshasa the whole mood began to change. A great gaiety took
over. 'The many open-air Masses were joyous celebrations,' says
Hebblethwaite. 'The invitation "Let us pray" was almost everywhere the signal for the tom-toms to beat out, solemnly and rever-
ently, and the offertory procession provided a chance for yet more
song and dance.' On the political side he never descended to details.
He told the diplomatic corps in Nairobi that Africa 'could and should
be allowed to solve its own problems without interference from
outside'. He seemed to look to a non-aligned Africa from which the
influence of the superpowers has been excluded. Again, he was
equally hard on the 'consumerism' of the West and the 'materialism'
of Communism. He attacked corruption of all kinds with unfailing

John Paul II is greeted by
African tribal chiefs.

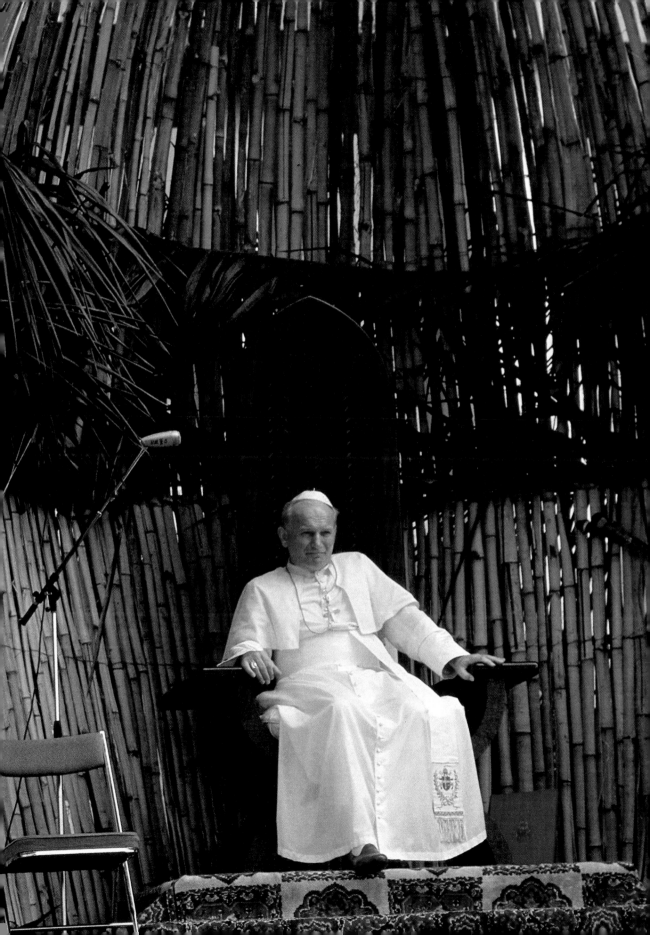

resolution. At the end of his journey, he summed up his impressions: 'For ten days,' he said, 'I have been the astonished and thunderstruck witness of the vitality of the young Churches in Africa. I invite the whole Church, especially the ancient Churches of Christendom, to look upon their sister Churches with esteem and confidence.' The Churches of Africa were henceforth to be treated as equals.

The deeper meaning of his visit to Africa was spelt out at length in *L'Osservatore Romano* the following year in what must be assumed to be an authorized interpretation. 'John Paul's journey in the Black Continent represents an ecclesiastical event of extraordinary significance.' African newspapers had defined it as 'a moral bomb'. 'The moral content and spiritual impact are fundamentally centred on the evangelization, on the development and consolidation of faith in the Continent, on the cultural adaptation of the Gospel, on the Africanization of the Church with respect to tradition and the unity of faith, on the family, and on vocations.' Some general words used by the Pope in various parts of the world were intended to have a special significance when he delivered them at Accra. 'I have come,' he said, 'to Africa – to carry out a mission entrusted to me by Divine Providence, the mission proclaiming the dignity and the fundamental equality of every human being and his right to live on in a world of justice, peace, brotherhood, and solidarity.'

A few sentences represent, in the summary, the message that a year later the Pope felt he had set out to deliver in Africa. 'Africa has something special to offer the world. . . . The young nations have much more to offer than simply a share of their natural resources or being a market for the products of the industrialized nations. Africa has preserved a place of honour for a long time.' The moment had come at last in which the importance due to Africa in the pursuit of international peace, justice and unity must be recognized. He went on to refer to Africa's original heritage which it must preserve and nourish. Africa must daily become more faithful to its own heritage, not out of opposition and antagonism towards others, but because it believes in the truth about itself. He warned the Africans to resist the easy temptation to copy or import ideas from the rest of the world, solely because they come from the so-called 'advanced' countries. The Pope asked: 'In what way are they advanced? Has not Africa, perhaps more than other continents, a sense of interior things called to determine man's life.' Africans should take advantage of 'true values coming from modern civilization' but they must find their own way under God to construct 'a new Africa, in accordance with Man's dignity and greatness'. No words that he used were more heartfelt than these: 'Africans: be yourselves.'

At 7 o'clock on the morning of 9 May, Pope John Paul II met

OPPOSITE During his stay in Accra, Ghana, Pope John Paul II had an historic meeting with Dr Robert Runcie, the Archbishop of Canterbury.

Dr Robert Runcie, recently appointed Archbishop of Canterbury, in Accra, capital of Ghana. It would have been impossible for two such benevolent figures not to enjoy a pleasant conversation, and hopefully embark on a fruitful discussion. Pope and Archbishop declared, 'The time is too short and the need too pressing to waste Christian energies pursuing old rivalries. The talents and resources of all the Christian strength must be shared if Christ be seen and heard effectively.' A basis of personal friendship and trust had been established upon which Pope and Archbishop intended to build in a fuller meeting in the future.

In a recent television interview, the Archbishop referred to the Pope as a Christ-centred humanist. He said that the Pope looks for a way of preventing the undervaluing of Christians in the world. Runcie stressed that the movement towards unity, though not uniformity, could be appropriately conducted 'in subordination to the Catholic vision of John Paul II.' All this augurs well for the Pope's visit in 1982.

At the end of June 1980, John Paul flew to Brazil. His tour of this country with the world's largest Catholic population, was the longest trip undertaken to date, lasting thirteen days. During this time he travelled over eighteen thousand miles and was proclaimed by twelve million people. The cities he visited ranged from the internationally popular Rio de Janeiro and the economically important São Paulo to the remote jungle city of Manaus. Thus the Pope witnessed some of the extremes of wealth which exist in the country. He was also plunged into the heart of Church/State problems for, during the previous twelve years, one hundred and twenty-two Bishops, priests and seminarians had been arrested or detained by the State. The dates of the tour were chosen to coincide with the tenth National Eucharistic Congress, held at Fortaleza.

Prior to the Pope's arrival, a document had been published by the Pastoral Commission of the Bishops' Conference. In this, criticism was levelled at the government for using 'all the material means at its command to favour the Pope's visit', while at the same time 'repressing the work being done by Church people committed to helping the oppressed according to Church teachings'. The document claimed that members of the Church had been subjected to death threats and kidnappings, ostensibly on account of their helping peasants to become aware of their rights. However, in a bid to improve its image, the government had announced an amnesty for approximately 3,000 prisoners. The Pope arrived against this backcloth of controversy. His visit was hailed by Cardinal Aloisio Lorscheider of Fortaleza as 'an affirmation of the Conference's pastoral program'.

OPPOSITE During his visit to South America, the Pope pauses at the foot of the massive statue of Christ the King at the top of Corcovado Hill, Rio de Janeiro.

On his arrival in Brasilia the Pope characteristically kneeled and kissed the soil, so reinforcing the missionary nature of his visit. In his opening speech, he described Brazil as 'the hope and joy of many Catholics in other countries' and referred to the land by its original names of the Portuguese colonial era, Vera Cruz (True Cross) and Santa Cruz (Holy Cross). He expressed the hope that Brazilians would work together peacefully to 'overcome imbalances and inequalities in justice', thereby setting an example for other countries. The Pope was met by the Brazilian President Joao Figueirado and his Cabinet, and various representatives of the Brazilian Church. The President said that his country was proud to receive 'a successor of St Peter' for the first time ever. John Paul II celebrated his first open-air Mass in Brazil in front of the ministry buildings, before a crowd of 500,000.

In Belo Horizonte, a mining city, John Paul II celebrated Mass for young people, as on so many of his visits. Before a large, enthusi-

The Pope talks with slum dwellers in Brazil.

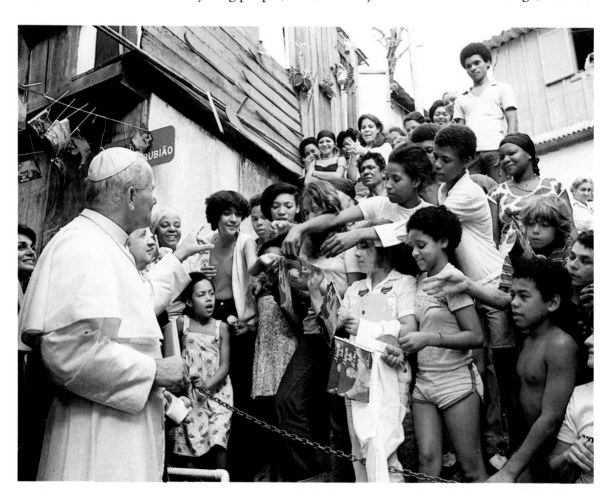

astic crowd who constantly shouted and chanted, the Pope pleaded for justice achieved through love and asked the young to avoid ideologies based on violence, hate and class warfare. He said, 'A young Christian ceases to be young, and certainly is not a Christian, when he lets himself be seduced by doctrines or ideologies that preach violence or hate. . . . It is indispensable to know how to conquer the temptation of the so-called consumer society, of the ambition to have always more, instead of trying to be more, of the ımbition to have more while others have less.'

In Rio de Janeiro, John Paul II celebrated another huge outdoor Mass in the Municipal Stadium. This was a strictly family occasion and he delivered an address on the threats which face the family in Brazil. He spoke of the 'sub-human living conditions, hygiene, health, education, conditions that can be found in the interior of the country and in the outskirts of the big cities, caused by unemployment and insufficient wages' as well as 'the general weakening of the family through lack of respect for human and Christian norms'.

Indeed, the next day John Paul II saw with his own eyes the sort of conditions he had described in his speech when he visited a slum parish on the edge of Rio de Janeiro. Here he called for social reform, and told the poor that they were 'especially close to God and his kingdom'. Then, to everyone's surprise, he gave away his papal ring to the poor people in the parish.

During the two days he spent in Rio de Janeiro, the Pope ordained seventy new priests at the Maracana Soccer Stadium, stressing that their role as priests was not that 'of a doctor, of a social worker, of a politician or a union leader' but an essentially spiritual one. He also met Brazilian academics, writers and artists representing the intellectual community. He spoke of the way in which culture could stimulate greater love in society but warned that people should avoid imposing their culture on 'populations that are economically and politically weaker'. The Pope also addressed members of the Latin American Bishops' Council and representatives of the laity.

Before he left Rio de Janeiro, the Pope said, as he stood at the foot of the famous statue named Christ the Redeemer and located on top of Corcovado Hill, that Rio de Janeiro was a city of 'life and joy, but . . . also a web of affliction and suffering, of violence and unfriendliness, of hatred, evil and sin'.

The next city to be visited was industrial São Paulo. Here John Paul addressed a group of 150,000 workers. He called on the workers of Brazil and the world to unite in creating a more just society. During the course of his speech the Pope was able to call on his own experience as a worker to reinforce his words. Speaking of the manual worker's condition, he said he knew 'its greatness and harshness, its hours of joyfulness and its moments of anguish. . . . Therefore I invite you, Christian workers, my brothers and sisters, to begin to celebrate in joyfulness and friendship what Jesus offers to one and all of us: the faith. . . . It is not a luxury reserved for the rich.' And in words that echoed his speeches in Ireland he continued, 'The common good of society will ever be the new name of justice. It cannot be obtained through violence, because violence destroys what it seeks to create. The changes demanded for there to be a just social order ought to be achieved through constant action along the path of peaceful reforms.'

One of the highlights of the trip came when John Paul II travelled to the small town of Aparecida for the consecration of the new Basilica which is claimed to be the largest Catholic church in the world after St Peter's in Rome. In his discourse here the Pope preached 'love and devotion to Mary'.

Before proceeding to the northeast and the Amazon, the Pope visited the cities of Porto Alegre and Curitiba. He told the inhabitants that their cities, composed of many different nationalities from Portuguese to Japanese, provided an excellent example of ethnic groups living together in harmony.

The final few days of John Paul's gruelling trip to Brazil were spent in the northeast of Brazil in some of the country's poorest states. Here he addressed lepers, farm workers and slum dwellers and reminded them never to lose sight of their human dignity. The purpose of many of his speeches was to recall the rights which every citizen should expect from its government: the right to life, to security, to work, to a home, to health, to education, to religious expression.

At Salvador, John Paul II tackled the theme of popular religiosity saying, 'Popular religious demonstrations, purified of their negative values, of all superstitions and magic, are without doubt a providential means of preserving the masses in their adhesion to the faith of their ancestors and to the church of Christ'. He said that no one should laugh at popular religion. This was a reference to Afro-Brazilian animist cults which mix Christianity with African rites, and prevail throughout northeast Brazil.

The Pope again visited slum areas and spoke to lepers. When he stopped over at Teresina, in one of the very poorest states, he told those with power, education and material goods to 'Take up – fully, unreservedly and irrevocably – the cause of your brothers who are trapped in poverty'. He pleaded for solidarity, saying that 'All men are equal in the eyes of God'.

In Belem, at the mouth of the River Amazon, the Pope visited a leprosarium, where he was moved to tears by welcoming remarks

made by one of the lepers. The man described the Pope's visit as just 'one more blessing' saying that 'the blessings we have received from God and Jesus Christ have been innumerable.' This visit was followed by an open-air Mass where the Pope again preached devotion to the Virgin Mary. Half a million people attended the meeting, a crowd typical of John Paul's trip to Brazil.

Before the Pope arrived in Fortaleza, where he was to open the National Eucharistic Congress, tragedy struck when a vast crowd poured into the soccer stadium where he was scheduled to speak later in the day. Several people were killed and many injured as the crowd surged into the stadium after being held back by a closed gate for some hours. However, the tragedy did not dampen the enthusiasm of the crowd that was waiting for the Pope. They still brandished banners and sang before he arrived.

During the course of his homily, John Paul II declared that 'the Church has not and will not ever cease to proclaim the fundamental

John Paul II prays with Amazonian Indians in their traditional dress.

rights of man: the right to settle freely in one's own country, to have a country, to emigrate within and outside the country for legitimate reasons, to be able to have a full family life, to count on the goods necessary for life, to preserve and develop one's own ethnic, cultural and linguistic patrimony, to profess publicly one's own religion, to be recognized and treated in accord with the dignity of one's person in any circumstance.' He added that life is a continuous series of encounters with Christ, including the Christ who is present in others, 'especially the poor, the weak, the marginalized'.

The Pope visited the River Amazon city of Manaus while staying in Fortaleza. Here he listened as Indian leaders complained about maltreatment. As he read from a text, John Paul II asked politicians to recognize the rights of the Indians. They gave him gifts of bows and arrows and bone necklaces.

The Pope spoke to members of the Brazilian Bishops' Conference, saying that, although the Church could be linked to revolutionary social reform, political violence could not be condoned. He spoke on evangelization, liturgy, catechetics, priestly and religious vocations, youth formation and popular religiosity.

By the time the Pope left Brazil for Rome he had visited thirteen cities in only thirteen days. *The Universe* described the tour as 'surely the most extraordinary papal journey in history'. He had spoken out for a more just distribution of wealth; and urged the poor to do everything within their power to ensure that they obtain rights owing to them by the government. His visit was, according to *The Universe*, 'an accusation of the Brazilian Government's criminal neglect'. Undoubtedly, many Christians had been shaken out of their complacency.

The weekend visit to Paris which John Paul II made at the end of May cannot be compared with the colossal African and Brazilian ventures, but in the event it seemed well worthwhile. The visit was undertaken against a depressing background of declining Church attendance. Attendance at Mass had fallen by more than three-fifths in the previous fifteen years. Once again, it is difficult to estimate the long-term effect of the visit but it had features which gave the Pope much legitimate satisfaction.

John Paul had looked at his programme a fortnight before he arrived in Paris and noticed there was no meeting with intellectuals. 'Everywhere I go I meet intellectuals, arrange a meeting with intellectuals.' A number of intellectuals were therefore invited to meet him at breakfast. We are told that he confined himself to asking them questions, and in particular, 'What do you think of the way the world is going?' This fits in with Jon Snow's impression that the Pope was far more interested in others and their opinions than in

OPPOSITE Wherever he goes, the Pope delivers a carefully thought-out address.

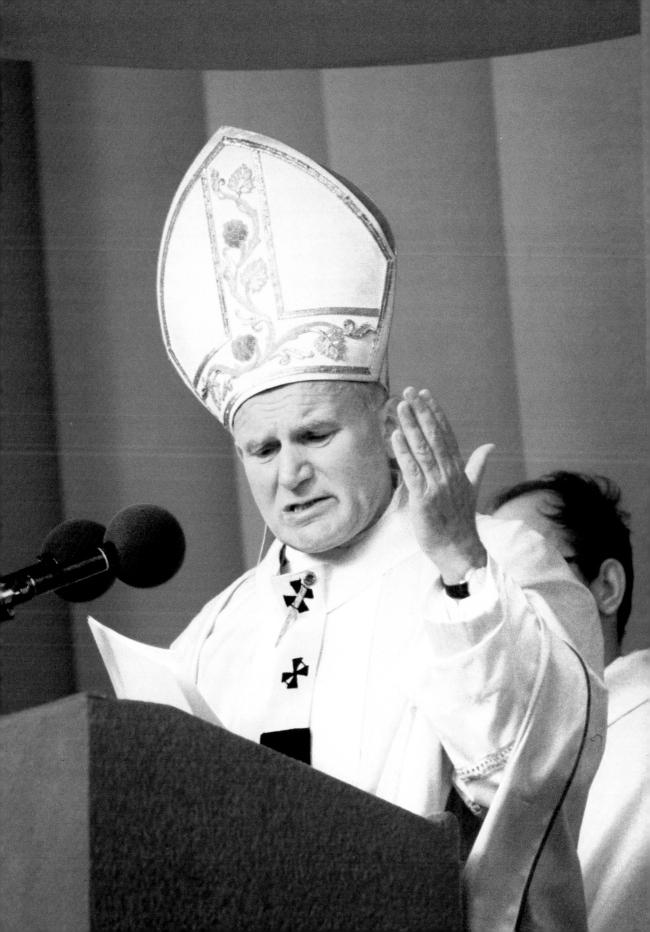

relating what he, the Pope, thought about matters. His insatiable
intellectual curiosity means that John Paul has a genuine interest in
the view of all human beings, particularly those who might have
something to convey to him in the world of ideas. Peter Hebblethwaite comments that the Pope seemed to have an outmoded image
of France. The three points of one of his homilies, 'Work, family and
the nation' were unhappily close to the model of the Pétain regime.
But, the day after making this speech, the Pope was equally emphatic
in proclaiming liberty, equality and fraternity as fundamental
Christian ideas.

Once more his meeting with young people was an unqualified
success. 50,000 youngsters gathered to meet him. John Paul had said
that he wanted a dialogue with them and the young people responded
by coming up to the microphone to question the Pope on his views
and statements. In his replies, the Pope celebrated youth as the hope
of the future. Once again, this man of immense intellectual powers
had found the way to the heart.

The Pope's last journey abroad in 1980 was to Germany. The
reason for the visit was the celebrations of the seven-hundredth
anniversary of the death of St Albert the Great, the master of St
Thomas Aquinas. There were a number of reasons for anxiety over
the success of the visit. The recent publications of the German

John Paul II talking to
French scouts.

OPPOSITE (above) The Pope
drives through the rue de
Bac on his weekend visit to
Paris in 1980; (below) The
Pope in the Champs Elysées,
Paris.

Bishops had been unfriendly to Luther, 'whose uncontrollable anger and polemical spirit blinded him to Catholic truth. His condemnation was inevitable.' The German Bishops tried to undo the mischief but it proved to be too late. This was the first encounter between the Germans and the Polish Pope. Wojtyla's wartime experiences in German-occupied Poland could hardly have failed to leave their mark on him. Large numbers of Germans had been driven from their homes in what was now Poland. It was, indeed, a delicate situation.

On Saturday, 15 November, Cologne Cathedral was filled with four thousand scientists, academics and students to hear the Pope deliver a lecture on St Albert the Great. Max Scheler, the subject of his second doctoral thesis, had been a professor in Cologne in the 1920s and the German style of intellectuality had always appealed to the Pope. He presented St Albert the Great as a thinker whose method of uniting faith and reason was of prime significance for the present age. The theme of his lecture was the need for a new alliance between faith and science and a new humanism for the third millenium. On the following Wednesday, the Pope made a similar appeal for a new alliance between the Church and artists, faith and culture. His words and ideas sprang from his own years of commitment to the causes he spoke about: theology, philosophy, the theatre and poetry. It is difficult to think of anyone else who could have spoken with such authority on theoretical ideas based on practical experience.

Any discussion about ecumenism would be of central importance. A meeting was arranged with representatives of the German evangelical church in Mainz at 8 o'clock the following morning. When he spoke, the Pope's words were a masterpiece of ecumenical diplomacy. He showed at once an expert knowledge of Luther's life and of the Epistle to the Romans which Luther had described as the heart of the New Testament. 'We have all,' said the Pope, 'in the spirit of Luther sinned. We cannot therefore judge each other. Jesus Christ is the salvation of us all. Through him the Father grants us pardon, justification, grace and eternal life. We must all confess these truths.' At the end of the speech the evangelical churchmen were left uncertain as to what, if any, difference remained between John Paul's approach to Luther and their own. It was a *tour-de-force* delivered as always from a background of prolonged meditation. If the points that he placed before his audience were carefully selected, that did not mean that his heart and mind were not fully absorbed in the spirituality they left behind them.

Finally he visited the old people in Munich Cathedral. Hebblethwaite said, 'His address was a prose poem which compared old age to the season of autumn. The senses are less acute, and the body no longer obeys the mind so readily. New information is less easily

OPPOSITE On his visit to Germany, Pope John Paul II kneels and prays at the tomb of St Albert the Great, the master of St Thomas Aquinas.

The Pope meets the people
of Germany.

assimilated, and the memory begins to play tricks. The world of
economics and politics becomes baffling and strange, and even the
Church is no longer what it used to be. Death itself takes on the
form of a consolation and a longed-for release from imprisonment.
For this world is not our true and definitive home.' 'It was deeply
felt,' said Hebblethwaite, 'beautifully expressed, profoundly Slav in
its melancholy, and entirely appropriate.'

There were two other important events in 1980: the Dutch Synod
and the Family Synod. The Dutch Synod was held inside the Vatican
where the curial participants were in the majority. The official purpose of the Synod was to consider the pastoral work of the Church
in the Netherlands. The Dutch Bishops at that point were known to
be seriously disunited. Four of the seven Bishops had strongly supported the 'progressive' line taken by their Church since the Second
Vatican Council. Two were opposed to it. Cardinal Willebrands
occupied a middle position. When the Bishops emerged from the

Synod on 31 January, they seemed to have rediscovered the lost communion. They paid unstinting tribute to John Paul, who had participated fully in their deliberations. The lengthy document which emerged reinforced the distinction between the people and the hierarchy, between the laity and the ordained ministry. The Dutch Bishops were persuaded to abandon 'liberal' policies that most of them had been committed to for the last fifteen years. Afterwards, commentators found it impossible to agree about the result of the Synod: some thought that it had been an enormous victory for the Pope, and that the Dutch Bishops had finally given way all too easily.

If the outcome of the Dutch Synod is surrounded in some confusion, it was impossible to ignore the conflicting opinions on the success of the Family Synod which took place from 26 September to 25 October 1980.

The Synod met to discuss 'the role of the Christian family in the modern world'. According to Peter Hebblethwaite, it began with high hopes and ended in confusion and a mood of frustration. The two hundred and sixteen Synod members at any rate emerged smiling; they said that the Synod had been a remarkably successful event, and that they had learned a great deal especially in their discussion groups and had gained a keener sense of the universality of the Church. Observers wondered whether they were not simply whistling to keep their courage up.

Five major themes emerged from early discussions. Firstly, there was a plea for a positive approach to sexuality and marriage. Cardinal O'Fiaich, for example, called for a recognition of the equality of the loving and procreative values of marriage. Secondly, there was a call for another look at the encyclical *Humanae Vitae* which had rejected artificial birth control so emphatically. Cardinal Hume spoke of those for whom natural as opposed to artificial methods of birth control do not seem to be the only solution. Thirdly, Archbishop Worlock expressed the hope that Catholics who were divorced and had remarried and yearned for the sacraments would be given sympathetic consideration. He was speaking after the experience of the National Pastoral Conference held in Liverpool. There was much support for his viewpoint. Fourthly, there was a call for a recognition of the merits of the feminist movement. Finally, African Bishops pleaded for greater freedom to assimilate some of their traditional marriage customs into the liturgy. Certainly, if the Pope had been a British Minister of the Crown answering a debate in Parliament, he would not have had a more formidable collection of opinions to reply to.

In the eyes of many his performance was disappointing. I am

convinced from a long talk with Archbishop Worlock that the nature of his final oration was misinterpreted by many in the Western world.

In the first place, the Pope was *not* replying to the debate; he was summing up the discussion, offering some comments and clarifications and calling attention to some things the Synod had recommended. In the second place, what the Pope actually said was much less negative than his progressive critics seemed to suggest. With regard to birth control, he indeed confirmed the ruling of *Humanae Vitae* but only in the sense that he pointed to this as the overwhelming opinion of the Synod. He firmly restated the current ruling of the Church on the access of divorced Catholics to the Eucharist. But he laid enormous stress on the obligation of all Catholics to continue to treat divorced persons who had remarried as baptized members of the Church requiring the understanding and support of the Catholic community, and still required to play their part in that community. He brought many in that situation much consolation and encouraged them to return to the Church.

In December 1981 the Pope reaffirmed the positions adopted in his commentary on the Family Synod. Reconciliation in the sacrament of penance which would open the way to the Eucharist can only be granted to those who are ready to live as brother and sister. But he lays extreme emphasis on the fact that those involved are to be treated as members of the Church.

Whether or not the representatives of Britain fared well in the Family Synod, there can be no question about the enormous success of the visit to the Pope by Her Majesty the Queen on 17 October. She and Prince Philip were played in by the Vatican Band with a rousing march, composed by one of its members and called 'Simplicity'. The goodwill escalated during the short visit. The Pope had forty minutes alone with the Queen and Prince Philip. Although they may have mentioned the subject of Ireland in their private discussions, it was not referred to in their public addresses. Someone present during the wider session told me that at first he felt that they were weighing each other up, but that by the end of the meeting an unqualified mutual trust had been established.

The Queen welcomed the visit that the Pope is making to Britain in 1982. She made it clear that he was coming to see the 'Roman Catholic Community' in Great Britain 'where some four million [*sic*] of my people are members of the Roman Catholic Church' (five million is a figure often mentioned). The Pope's visit, in other words, would not be a State visit like her visit to him, but she emphasized the contribution that it could make to the growing movement of unity between the Christian Churches throughout the world.

OPPOSITE The meeting of Pope John Paul II and Queen Elizabeth II whom he officially received at an audience in the Vatican on 17 October 1980.

(above) The Queen and Prince Philip walk along the corridors of the Vatican on their way to their meeting with Pope John Paul II; (below) John Paul II and the Queen during the audience.

The smiles on the faces of John Paul II, the Queen, and Prince Philip show the warmth of their meeting.

'We pray that His Holiness's visit to Britain may enable us all to see more clearly those truths which both unite and divide us in a new and constructive light.'

The Pope, in his much longer reply, paid tribute to the great simplicity and dignity with which 'Your Majesty bears the weight of your responsibilities'. He spoke about Britain with a warmth no less sincere. 'In the person of your Majesty,' the Pope said, 'I render homage to the Christian history of your people, as well as to their cultural achievements. The ideals of freedom and democracy, anchored in your past, remain challenges for every generation of upright citizens in your land. . . . In this century your people have repeatedly endeavoured to defend these ideals against aggression.'

He spoke of his 'pastoral visit to the capital of Great Britain' with keen anticipation. He looked forward also to greeting with fraternal respect and friendship all people of goodwill. The whole event could not have passed off more happily.

Chapter 7

The Way of the Cross
1981

J OHN PAUL'S REIGN soared to new heights in 1981 with a twelve-day trip to the Far East including the Philippines and Japan. But it sank to appalling depths with an attempt on his life in May, which all too nearly succeeded.

The year began, however, with the Pope meeting twelve Nobel Prizewinners in science, chemistry, economics and physics, who were in Rome for a two-day conference on the theme 'Man among Hopes and Threats'. Speaking to the Prizewinners, John Paul II declared that 'the opposition between science and faith' was a thing of the past: 'A new period has begun: the efforts of scientists and theologians must now be directed to developing a constructive dialogue.' He warned them, however, that 'scientific progress is not always accompanied by a similar improvement in man's living conditions'. He said that the criterion for scientific endeavour ought to be 'the criterion of serving man, the whole man, in the whole of his spiritual and bodily subjectivity'. The winners were described by the Pope as 'watchful sentinels on the paths of progress'. As such they should denounce 'any form of intervention on man or his life environment that would be seen to be an attack on his dignity or his inalienable rights'.

The visit to the Far East occupied twelve days of the following month, spanned a distance of 23,000 miles and involved greeting ten million people. It took the Pope to Japan, never before visited by a Pope, and to the oppressed Philippine Islands.

He had set the tone of the visit to the Far East in Karachi, when he had addressed a throng of people, half Catholic, half Muslim, using a direct ecumenical approach with words such as: 'Don't forget that Abraham is the father of the Jews, the Christians and the Muslims.' The ecumenical theme was sustained throughout the visit. At Davao, on the island of Mindanao, the Pope pleaded with Muslim officials to end the nine-year-old guerilla war: 'Is it not right to imagine that, in the Philippines, the Muslims and the Christians are travelling on the same ship, for better or worse, and that in the storms which sweep the world the safety of each individual depends

OPPOSITE In the Philippines the Pope is presented with a model boat by a small boy.

168

(right) The Pope celebrates
an open-air Mass in Manila;
(below) The joyous welcome
given to the Pope on his
arrival in the Philippines.

upon the efforts and co-operation of all?'

But the main thrust of his message was delivered in Manila. Speaking in a televised address to an estimated thirty-five million people, John Paul spoke fearlessly for human rights: 'Any apparent conflict between the needs of security and of the citizens' basic rights must be resolved according to the fundamental principle, always upheld by the Church, that social organization exists only for the service of man and for the protection of his dignity; that it cannot claim to serve the common good when human rights are not safeguarded.' He met President Marcos of the Philippines and praised the President's decision to lift martial law, saying that it augured well for the future of the Philippines. He warned the anti-government wing of the Church there to avoid interfering in politics, reminding them of their roles in society: 'You are priests and religious. You are not social or political leaders or officials of a temporal power.'

The Pope's reception in the Philippines was as warm as might be expected from a strongly Catholic community; wherever he went, crowds of half a million assembled. In Japan, his reception was predictably cooler. His arrival in Tokyo did nothing to ease the frenetic

The Pope's compassion for the sick is expressed in this encounter with a handicapped child in the Philippines.

pace of life in the bustling metropolis, and only a small crowd turned up to meet him. Though smaller in size, the Catholic community of Japan is still dear to the Pope; he referred to the estimated 500,000 Catholics among a population of 117 million as *Pusillus Grex* (a tiny flock).

During his visit, the Pope said Mass at Hiroshima and Nagasaki, where 100,000 people perished in 1945. The prayer he offered drew together the themes of peace, brotherhood and Christian love: 'May Almighty God in His mercy never allow the destructive power of the Hiroshima and Nagasaki atomic bombs to be released again in human history. . . . Here where the memory and signs of the explosion are living and obvious, the words of Christ cannot fail to take on a particular vividness: Peace be with you.' He met and spoke with survivors from the explosions.

The Pope's trip to the Far East led many people to reconsider their opinions of him. An editorial in *The Universe* on 20 February 1981 declared that, 'Those who have pigeon-holed Pope John Paul II as a dyed-in-the-wool reactionary will have to think again after his visit to the Philippines.' *The Universe* went on to describe him as neither left- nor right-wing, but 'that most unfashionable of political

During his visit to Japan the Pope had a long talk with Emperor Hirohito.

(left) When he visited Hiroshima, the Pope delivered a condemnation of war; *(below)* The Pope visits one of the victims of the nuclear holocaust in Hiroshima.

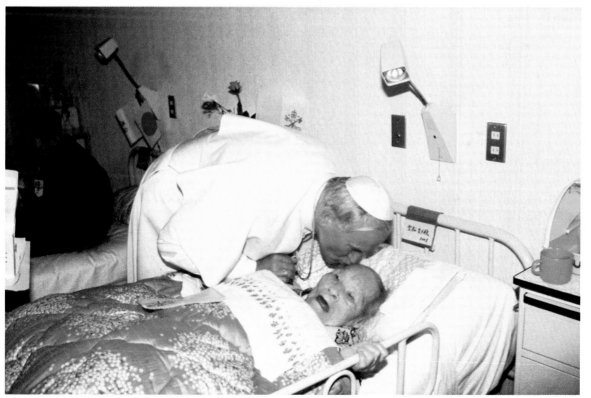

creatures, a Christian.' In re-stating his concern for basic rights and freedoms of the individual, the Pope was echoing one of the themes emerging from the Second Vatican Council: that the dignity of man is given to him by Almighty God. Politics, therefore, become insignificant, 'except in so far as they act as vehicles through which man's dignity is either enhanced or degraded'.

A second trip abroad was originally planned for 1981: the Pope was to visit Switzerland in June. The Swiss Catholic Bishops and the International Labour Organization (ILO) had invited John Paul II to attend meetings in Geneva. Other towns were also on the agenda. On 13 May all such plans were dashed brutally to the ground.

It was 5.19 p.m. The Pope in his white jeep had just completed his first round of contact with the crowd at a General Audience. He had been waving affectionately to groups of children and had almost stopped at times to talk to pilgrims and visitors, 'drawn up' in Peter Nichols's fine phrasing in *The Times*, 'to sense the aura of protective strength which John Paul II was so adept at giving to the crowds who flocked to see him.' His jeep was moving towards the chair in front of the steps of the Basilica where the Pope would sit to read his address. Suddenly a succession of shots rang out. The Pope was still for a moment, then he fell. An eye-witness reported that, 'He was clutching his chest as he went down. He never changed his expression. After he fell to the ground, he changed his expression with some pain, but the painful expression quickly disappeared and he appeared calm.' He fell into the arms of his faithful secretary. An American woman and a Jamaican woman were also hit.

Without hesitation, the driver took the jeep back into the Vatican. A few minutes later an ambulance removed the wounded Pope to hospital where the last rites were administered and an operation lasting five hours was performed. At 10.20 a Hospital spokesman announced that 'an operation was carried out successfully. There were no particular problems. The Pope lost less than a litre of blood. The main risk now is infection. But the risk is limited because the Pope is a healthy man.' The Pope had been still conscious when taken to the operating theatre. He asked in a bewildered voice, 'How could they?' As soon as he recovered, he immediately forgave the assassin.

The man in question was a young Turk, Mehmet Ali Agca, who had been imprisoned for his role in killing the editor of an important Turkish daily newspaper, the *Milliyet*. In November 1979 he had escaped from a top-security prison in Istanbul and sent a letter to the *Milliyet*. In the letter he said, 'My sole purpose in escaping is to kill the Pope.' At the time, the Pope was in Turkey on an official visit. Naturally, security measures were intense.

Two remarkable
photographs of the attempted
assassination of Pope John
Paul II on 13 May 1981.

A spokesman at the Gemelli Clinic gives the Press the daily report on the condition and progress of the Holy Father after the assassination attempt.

For nearly two years, Agca evaded the police. For a time he was said to be living quite openly amongst the many immigrant workers in West Germany. Then, nine days before the assassination attempt, the Turkish government warned Italian police that Agca was in Italy, carrying a false passport. Yet the Italian police did not locate him until the damage had been done and the Pope was lying seriously ill in hospital, struck down by the bullets from Agca's gun.

Guesswork surrounding the attack on the Pope's life has been rife. Months later, newspapers were still speculating on the motives of the gunman. The general consensus of opinion, however, was that the gunman was not working alone. Sufficient evidence has not been gathered to support any of the numerous theories that were put forward. It was suggested that the 'jackal' was working for the KGB. In September 1981, the *Guardian* reported that the Vatican was 'convinced' that the Soviet Secret Service had had a hand in the attack, 'aimed at silencing the Pope at a sensitive time in Poland'. Yet West

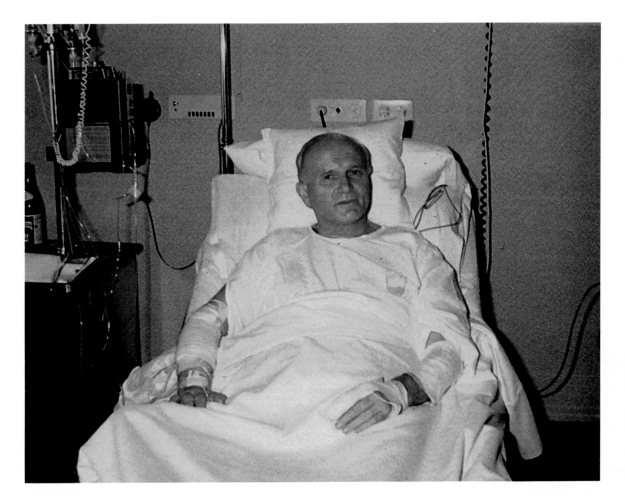

Germany's anti-terrorist agency viewed such reports as pure 'speculation'. When the Court of Assize in Rome convicted Agca of trying to kill the Pope, the report giving reasons for sentencing Agca to life imprisonment stated: 'The attack against John Paul II was not the work of a delirious ideologue or a criminal who did everything by himself. He was the fruit of a complex plot orchestrated by hidden minds interested in destabilization. But honesty requires us to admit that the evidence gathered has not permitted the State to discover the people behind the conspiracy . . .' And so the speculation continues.

On 19 May international medical specialists who had been invited to Rome for consultation about the Pope's condition issued a reassuring communiqué. They said they had come at the invitation of the medical team who were treating the Pope. They had been provided with every facility and had been 'privileged to examine the Pope'. They went on to state: 'The emergency care was most com-

The Pope in the Gemelli Clinic shortly after the attempt on his life.

John Paul II appears at the
the window of the Gemelli
Clinic to acknowledge the
crowds who gathered there
every day.

plete and effective. The surgical care was excellent, as has been the
intensive medical management since that time. In spite of the extremely serious nature of his wounds the Pope, at the end of the
sixth post-operative day, looks well and his vital signs are returning
towards normal. He is taking nourishment by mouth and has been
able to sit up. While we are pleased by his progress to date, it is clear
that even a patient as remarkably fit as the Pope will require a prolonged period of recuperation.'

On 31 May, after nineteen days at the Gemelli Hospital, Pope
John Paul returned to the Vatican. For the first time since the attempt
on his life, the Holy Father had recorded a Sunday address, this time
to more than 15,000 faithful gathered in St Peter's Square. He had
something to say on this occasion that was very close to his heart. No
sickness, however extreme, would have prevented him delivering
the message: 'I exalt you particularly,' he said, 'to unite in spirit with
the reverent homage of prayers that Poland is offering for the soul
of its late Primate – Cardinal Stefan Wyszynski, so greatly appreciated and loved by all.' The Lord had 'called him to Himself' the
previous Thursday. He referred to the death of one who was for over
thirty years 'the keystone of the unity of the Church in Poland'. It
had awakened in the Pope a host of memories and sentiments. 'They
make me feel very close to all those who will this afternoon pay him
the devout and last tribute.'

The flow of messages did not cease. On 14 June he delivered a
special 'thank you to youth' in all parts of the world. 'Today,' he
said, 'I wish to address my thanks – my special thanks – to the young

OPPOSITE The Pope leaves
the Gemelli Clinic to return
to the Vatican after the
assassination attempt.

On his return to the Vatican, the Pope was greeted by members of his household.

OPPOSITE Daily at noon from a window of his apartment, the Pope says the Angelus with pilgrims in St Peter's Square. This is his first appearance since the assassination attempt.

of the whole world, who have been particularly close to me in this period of suffering with their affection and their prayers. I am thinking, for example, of the young people of my Cracow, of my Rome, of those in Switzerland whom I should have met in the past days, and of the many others in various countries in the world who have wished to be spiritually close to me and all of whom it is difficult for me to name here.' The words that followed were deeply felt: 'Let them rest assured that their messages and their prayers have really been a support and comfort to me, because I have seen in them the true love that Christ revealed to us.'

But he was not yet out of the wood. On 20 June it was learned that he had had to return suddenly to hospital. The blood transfusions used during his operation had been infected and caused a relapse. During the late summer many Catholics in Britain doubted whether he would be well enough to visit this country in 1982. But from then on the news steadily improved.

An unusual view of Pope John Paul II at his summer residence of Castelgondalfo.

The historic encyclical *Laborem exercens* was to have been published on 15 May, in conjunction with the observance of the ninetieth anniversary of Leo XIII's great social encyclical *Rerum Novarum*. The assassination attempt postponed publication and enabled the Pope to spend much time re-writing it during the summer. It seems that increasing tension in Poland led him to bring out the Polish implications even more clearly. 'Christianity,' he wrote, 'seeks to have work permeated, in a certain sense, by a new life.' He went on to say that Christianity brought this about, 'by means of sanctification and prayer, by sharing in the creative and redemptive work of the Word, in the suffering – joy of work, realizing in this way the "paschal mystery of work".' The Pope announced the publication of this historic document on 13 September. *Laborem exercens* was published two days later.

The Pope's convalescence ended on 7 October. He resumed his Wednesday Audiences in St Peter's Square, moving freely, but within a more restrictive circle imposed by security considerations. After the Wednesday Audience, people all over Rome were saying to themselves: 'The Pope is himself again.'

On Thursday, 29 October, *The Times* carried the announcement: 'After months of uncertainty it was confirmed yesterday that Pope John Paul II will visit Britain next May. Cardinal Hume and Cardinal Gray of Edinburgh issued a statement yesterday in the light of a private audience with the Pope last Saturday: "Our preparations for the visit will now proceed."' The Pope had made a remarkable recovery. But people were asked to be 'sensitive to the need for preserving the good health of our visitor.' As Gerard Noel, editor of the *Catholic Herald* and a number of books on the Papacy, has told me, 'His experiences and his bravery make it likely that he will win many hearts on his coming visit. . . . But we too, presumably, must play our part.'

Pope John Paul II granted me a private audience at the Vatican on 2 December 1981. I took my place in the Audience Hall at 11 a.m. The vast audience of about 10,000 people, which included delegations from many countries, waited tensely. Then at the back of the Hall there was a sudden flurry. Among the throng a bulky figure in white could be seen making his way slowly forward. The Pope moved up the aisle, speaking to many and being spoken to by still more, some of them evidently feeling that to touch him was sufficient. Half way up the aisle, he paused and moved back again to speak, it seemed, to young people whom he felt that he might have neglected. Eventually he reached the platform. Messages of welcome were delivered by the many delegations. He replied in half a dozen languages, each group applauding fervently when they were mentioned. The theological meat was then offered. The Pope delivered an address to the people gathered in the Audience Hall. It was one in

The Pope at a relaxed audience for young Austrian pilgrims at Castelgondalfo, his summer residence, in September 1981.

a series on the Resurrection which he made through last winter.

To the surprise of the visitors from overseas a circus party then put on a dazzling display of acrobatics. As each performer finished his or her act, they came forward and received the Pope's benediction. Finally, he moved deliberately along the front row, bending with special solicitude, in the manner I remember so well on his Irish visit, over the disabled in their wheelchairs.

An hour later than scheduled, I was led into an interview chamber. The Holy Father entered quietly, moving without haste but covering the ground with speed, his physical power even more pronounced than I expected, his slight stoop also noticeable.

I had been advised that the Pope might resist any attempt to kiss his ring, but whether or not out of courtesy, he seemed to welcome the gesture. I ventured to say that it was very good of him to see me. He expressed what I took to be real pleasure in our meeting. They were conventional enough words but they carried complete conviction. He clearly felt it was good to meet someone who had come from England.

I had brought an illuminated letter from our parish priest and other members of the parish. The Pope asked me to convey his best wishes to 'all members of your parish and particularly your parish priest'.

Obviously I am unable to repeat in detail our conversation since it was a private audience. But I was able to retire from my talk with the Holy Father with his blessing upon my work. Indeed he quipped about the book written about him, 'It must have been a difficult job'; the last word was pronounced in the American fashion.

The overwhelming memory is of his gentleness. In my time, I have called on many prominent persons. Courtesy has been invariable, kindness has been common and an instinctive assertion of personality commoner still. There was nothing whatever of the attempt to impress in Pope John Paul II. He had spent the previous two-and-a-half hours giving and receiving benevolence. For the time being, he focused on me alone. I had been responding to the Pope's mass appeal wholeheartedly but from the periphery. Now for a short while, I was swept into his magic circle as everyone is who meets him face to face.

OPPOSITE Pope John Paul II with Lord Longford after his private audience in the Vatican in December 1981

Chapter 8

The Man and the Message

FIRST, LAST AND ALWAYS, comes Pope John Paul II's emphasis on Christ as the centre of all that matters. At the beginning of *Redemptor Hominis* (1979), he wrote: 'The Redeemer of man, Jesus Christ, is the centre of the Universe and of history.' It may be said that there is nothing new or original about these words. But the place they occupy in the encyclical gives us a clue as to the deepest convictions of Pope John Paul II. It is a sentiment which affects the Pope at all times in his life of prayer and just as continuously in his work for humanity. It must not be forgotten that the Pope we are dealing with here is a spiritual and not a political leader. His spiritual message, however, partly through the man himself, and partly through his unique position, cannot fail to affect the course of world history, even if that effect can never be measured.

The Pope presides over 739 million Catholics (at the last count), 18 per cent of the world's population. Peter Nichols is surely right in attributing to them a much larger share of influence, actual or potential, than that percentage suggests. More than half of the world's Catholics live outside Europe and North America. It is estimated that by the year 2,000 about 70 per cent of baptized Catholics will live in the Third World. Catholicism in England has grown from 0.3 per cent of the population to about 10 per cent today.

The Vatican, the smallest of states – it is about 108.5 acres in size – controls the world's largest religious community and, from the West's point of view, the most imposing. The man in charge of all this carries no ordinary responsibility.

But this is no ordinary man. I can think of no one living today who has such a varied range of accomplishments as Pope John Paul II. He is perhaps best known for the importance he attaches to the inherent dignity of the individual. His repeated references to 'the dignity of man' may have their origins in a number of the Pope's personal experiences: the years he spent as a worker in a quarry in wartime Poland; in the far more horrible suffering which he saw during the German occupation of Poland; in the agonized reaction to thirty-five years of Communist domination in Poland; in personal insights

OPPOSITE The Pope comforts the mother of a sick child.

186

Looking at the façade of St Peter's Basilica and the Bernini colonnade from St Peter's Square

arising from his spiritual and intellectual studies. Its expression has been seen most strikingly in his travels and meetings with people of every possible creed, class and colour over the world.

John Paul II refers almost as frequently to his belief in the principle of freedom. Freedom is a concept which means much to all of us though hardly the same to any two persons. It has a special implication for Pope John Paul II. He is imbued, obsessed is hardly too strong a word, with the conviction that each one of us has it in him or her at all times to make a fundamental choice between good and evil. He sees it as being in our power to become divine or devilish. In *Redemptor Hominis* are these sentences: 'Christ's union with man is power and the source of power, as St John stated so incisively in the prologue of his Gospel: "The word [that is Christ] gave power to become children of God".'

PREVIOUS PAGES A view of the Vatican from the cupola of St Peter's Basilica

The whole dignity of man rests on the divine potentiality contained in him. But it is only under conditions of freedom that that potentiality can be achieved. In the practical sphere. the twin ideas of freedom and human dignity lead on to the Pope's insistence on human rights which he has proclaimed with an ever-increasing urgency.

He has repeatedly been admired as a unifying force by his colleagues in episcopal discussions. It is a gift which would seem to come from the Pope's instinctive ability to understand the 'other man's' point of view. During his years in Cracow he enjoyed many discussions with young Marxists. He knew their case better than they did and won their esteem and affection. This same ability to interest himself in the opinion of others is recalled by Bishop Murphy O'Connor. In 1975, when the Bishop was head of the English College at Rome he thought that it would be edifying for the students to invite a possible future Pope to lunch. But Cardinal Wojtyla was far more interested in listening than in talking.

John Paul II's talent for communicating with young people has been seen time and again on his tours. Two young people have told me that it is an aspect of John Paul that they appreciate. Sue Davis, a twenty-two-year-old student at St Mary's College of Education, Strawberry Hill, gives an idea of the feelings the Pope arouses in his flock when she says: 'Even when I find myself disagreeing with what he says, as for instance on the subject of contraception, I do not think of him as laying down the law for me, but rather as trying to dialogue with me, inviting me to think out my position and be clear for the reasons for my attitude.' Mark Ward, a sixteen-year-old pupil at

The Pope in a happy moment with young admirers

The Pope toasting the miners of Terni. He has always felt an affinity with workers.

St William of York's School, Islington, has told me that 'when the Pope journeys round the world and speaks to people of different nationalities, everyone who is good and honest recognizes the good in him and responds to him. In our world today he is a great influence for good.'

The Pope, ever since his days in the quarry at the beginning of the 1940s, has been emotionally involved with 'the workers'. In the Pope's eyes, atheistic Marxism is the worst enemy of the workers; he believes that it will destroy their freedom entirely. He is speaking from all too bitter experience in Poland. He is, after all, the first Pope to have been involved throughout his career with the institution of a Communist State and society. He has had to live with Communism and it has been for him an unceasing struggle to make sure that Poland and the religion of Poland will not be submerged. The Pope claims, as Tom Burns, editor of the Catholic paper *The Tablet*, has pointed out, that 'The dignity and real freedom of men knows no frontiers, above all none within the European continent. The Pope's message to an arid and two-dimensional Marxism-Communism is clear: "Europe, bounded by its geographical frontiers, with its inheritance of culture and civilization, can assure its future only upon a basis of strong ethical principles and only if the

OPPOSITE John Paul II with Mother Teresa of Calcutta

The Pope with the then
President of the United
States, Jimmy Carter

creative penetration of the leaven of the Gospel is not crushed by
conquest and by the slavery of men and of nations." '

He insists in *Laborem exercens* on the priority at all times of the
workers; the Church must be the Church of the Poor. But at no
time does this lead him, as it so often leads progressive people, close
to the narrow line between left-wing democratic policies and Marxism. He reminds me in this respect of Ernest Bevin, whom I served
admiringly at one point during his Foreign Secretaryship in the
Labour government of 1945 to 1951. No one could have described
Bevin as anything but working-class; his heart lay with the workers
as inflexibly as does that of Pope John Paul II in a non-political sense.
But Bevin detested Communism and all forms of Marxism. I remember at a dinner at the Russian Embassy in 1947 Mr Molotov
suggested that Mr Bevin should study Marx in the commentary of
Hilferding. Bevin replied: 'I've studied Hilferding and I found him
tedious.'

It would be a mistake, however, to treat the present Pope as some

194

The Pope in a light-hearted mood in Africa

kind of diplomatic ally of the Atlantic alliance against the Eastern bloc. Brought up in Poland, it is possible that he finds the superficial ethical puritanism that he knew in Poland in some respects more congenial than the flagrant permissiveness of Western society. Some of us who live in the West will not be too sure exactly what the Pope is describing in our way of life that he finds so repulsive. We were accustomed a few years ago to complaints about our affluent society, but that phrase has not been much used lately. Our prevalent self-criticism is a complaint, not that we produce too much, but that we produce far too little.

In Ireland, John Paul II told the young people and indeed their elders to beware of the grave dangers of increasing prosperity. The standard of living of the Irish people was, until recent years, appallingly low. In spite of considerable progress in the last quarter of a century, the standard of living in Ireland has still not caught up with that in England. In his attack on consumerism, the Pope seems to have more than one idea in mind: firstly, the traditional perils of

The Pope administers a
baptism on his visit to Africa.

the rich set out explicitly in the Gospels; secondly, the careless or
arrogant use of consumer goods in Western societies. Someone who
knows the Pope's mind has used the awkward word 'throw-away-
ability' to explain his meaning. Like impatient children we grow
tired of our possessions, throw them away and rush off to acquire
new ones. That at least is how it strikes the Pope from Poland. The
wealthy countries obtain as large a share as possible of the world's
goods, indifferent to the effects of their greed on the undernourished
millions in the poorer nations of the world.

The Pope's denunciation of the Arms race, which is applauded vociferously and no doubt springs from his heart, is remarkably even-handed. Whatever his inner thoughts, he does not distinguish between the 'goodies' and the 'baddies' as most of us inevitably do in the West. Those of us in Britain who believe that multilateral disarmament is the only rational solution will have no excuse if we do not heed the Pope's strictures and re-double our efforts.

In the same way, his unqualified denunciation of Marxism in *Laborem exercens* gives little consolation to those who preach the doctrines of Adam Smith or defend the more old-fashioned kinds of capitalism or market economy. He acknowledges that large improvements have been made but he shows little enthusiasm for any system of free enterprise. The principle of the priority of labour over capital is for him a postulate of the order of social morality. 'But the many deeply desired reforms cannot be achieved by an *a priori* elimination of private ownership of the means of production.' Somehow or other, and he is not as precise as to the means, John Paul II believes that a system must be established of 'joint ownership of the means of work, a sharing by the workers in the management and/or profits of businesses'. This has been said before by previous Popes, but never with quite so much urgency. One begins to see that more and more a triple theme is emerging: family, work and culture.

Outside the family domain, it might seem reasonable to place John Paul II's political views on the left rather than the right, though he does not think in these categories, so familiar in Britain and other Western countries. In matters connected with the family, such as artificial birth control, and the more recent issue of access to the sacraments for divorced persons, he is 'traditional' rather than 'conservative'.

Cardinal Hume has also said that anything done by the Pope would be 'within the tradition'. He would be concerned at all times to preserve 'the deposit of faith'. He would stand, in good times and bad, for the affirmation of eternal Catholic principles and ideals. And perhaps that last word, 'ideals', gives the main clue to one of the two chief purposes of John Paul II's Papacy. Dr Huntston Williams states categorically that 'the Pope is an exponent of an entirely new ascetic ideal', a formidable claim when we bear in mind the two-thousand-year tradition of Catholic asceticism. Personally, I would present the Pope as an heroic figure, himself capable of spiritual and physical heroism, and pointing the way to others to follow his example: 'Be ye therefore perfect, as your Father in Heaven is perfect.' Rowanne Pascoe, editor of the Catholic newspaper *The Universe*, sums up his strengths: 'Despite, or perhaps because of, his lack of army divisions, the Pope is the one person who can be called a world leader. In an age of political pygmies he has taken over the moral leadership of

In his address to the United
Nations in 1979, the Pope
showed his incisive and
penetrating intellect.

the world. It does not appear to be a role he has set out to fill but
people have almost forced it upon him. They sense his goodness and
selflessness.'

There are other facets of his personality, other attributes of this
extraordinary man, which have been touched on earlier. The amazing
warmth of his personality, and a certain shyness at first meeting that
goes with it, and his exceptional gift of communicating with all
mankind, were never better illustrated than when he addressed the
United Nations Congress in 1979 with the words: 'I wish above all
to send my greetings to all the men and women living on this planet.
To every man and woman without exception whatever.' From any
other human being, even from some other Pope, those words would
have lacked credibility; they would hardly have rung true. But from
him they seemed altogether in character and appropriate.

His devotion to the blessed Virgin Mary is a fundamental part of
him. He concluded the Lenten Addresses which he delivered in 1976
at the request of Pope Paul VI with some lyrical pages in her honour.
It would be difficult to connect his Marian devotion directly with his
philosophy, or even the main strands of his theology. But it is impossible to think of him without it. In this respect he shares, no doubt,
in a fervent Polish tradition. His love of the Virgin Mary goes back
to his earliest years.

OPPOSITE The Pope places a
candle before the statue of
the Virgin Mary to whom he
has always had the strongest
devotion.

It is unlikely that his professed attitude to women will fully com-
mend itself to advanced feminists. Yet those who know him best will

OPPOSITE The Pope is never happier than when speaking to the people.

insist that he is trying at all times 'to upgrade motherhood', and not downgrade the work of women outside the home and the religious life. What he has to say on this matter in *Laborem exercens* must be studied textually. His central contention is that there is a certain role in motherhood beyond the act of childbearing which cannot be fulfilled by men, and in which women can fulfil themselves as well as maintaining the existence of society. This does not exclude fulfilment women may find outside the home in addition to family duties.

The Pope dwells often on the first chapters of Genesis, where he finds expressed the supreme love of God the Creator. He finds there also the equality of the first man and the first woman. It may be said that it was the first woman who led the first man astray. But the Pope leaves that antithesis for a higher synthesis (my words, not his) in his undying devotion to the Virgin Mary, who compensates superabundantly for the errors of Eve.

The Pope performs the Stations of the Cross at the Colisseum in Rome as part of the Easter ceremonies during which he made a plea for world peace.

I asked one of his oldest friends what led the Pope to become a priest. Various explanations are offered in the text, but I was told that the present Pope's long-standing depth of prayer should be regarded as the crucial factor. Should he, then, be regarded as a mystic? Yes,

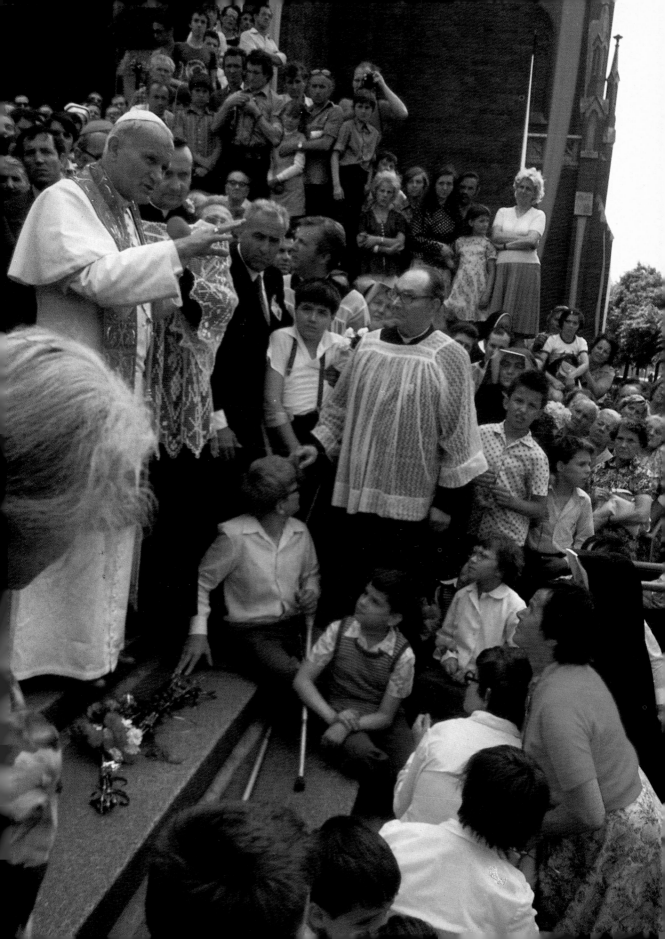

After the assassination attempt on his life, the Pope was visited by his friend, the former Archbishop of Canterbury, Dr Ramsey.

assuredly. It is interesting that St John of the Cross, on whom John Paul II wrote his first thesis, and also the modern saint, Theresa of Avila, to whom he has always been much devoted, were 'liberal mystics' in painful conflict with the orthodoxy of their time. The Pope, I should add, always writes his encyclicals on his knees. It is impossible to separate his immense intellectuality from his prayerfulness in all his life and work.

It is difficult to assess the short- or the long-term effect in any recognizable political sense of his numerous addresses to millions of enthusiastic listeners throughout the world. Can anything positive be said about Vatican diplomacy at the present time? The Vatican's strategy is simple enough: the preservation of the right of worship of Catholics, at all times and in all countries, and, of course, the pursuit of peace and, ever more insistently, of human rights and the welfare of the poor. But the day-to-day tactics are veiled in much secrecy. His influence has been more obvious in Poland, because he is the greatest of living Poles. Everyone can appreciate the enormous gain in self-confidence that the Poles acquired through his visit, and the fact that it was organized on a vast scale by the people rather than by their rulers.

This book goes to press on 1 January 1982. Today, in his New Year message, the Pope has given the clearest possible support to Solidarity. He has said that the word 'Solidarity' shows us the endeavour which aims for justice and peace. We can be fairly certain that Pope John Paul II will pursue three objectives: to hearten the Polish people and to identify himself with them at all times; to restrain them from any course of violence; and to promote tirelessly discussions between the Church, the government and the trade union movement.

The 'Polishness' of the Pope is central to his Papacy. No one doubts that John Paul II is a Pole to the depth of his being. I asked an old Polish friend of his what special characteristics marked out the Pope as distinctively Polish. In the first place, he said, poetry. All Poles are natural poets. Karol Wojtyla in his irresistible urge to write poetry is a true Pole. But next he singled out what he called a special cordiality towards the individual. A Pole, he said, does not like a visitor to leave without giving him a gift, however small. The present Pope is restrained with difficulty from asking everyone who comes

The Pope listens attentively to Lech Walesa, the leader of the Polish Trade Union, Solidarity, at a private audience on 15 January 1981.

to see him to stay to lunch or dinner. At this point, my Polish friend insisted on calling for morning coffee and persuaded me to eat some Polish cakes. It is well known that the Pope's first action after his election was to call on his old friend, now Archbishop Deskur, who was in hospital suffering from a severe stroke. It is not so well known that he decided that in the year of the disabled he would ask a disabled person to lunch every Sunday. Archbishop Deskur duly received an invitation each Sunday.

Now the Pope comes to Britain. It is safe to say that he will be enormously welcome. There will, no doubt, be a powerful curiosity at work, because this is the first time a Pope has ever visited Britain. Wherever John Paul travels, he is treated like a superstar and his visit will live up to expectations. Sister Gemma Brennan IVBM, as one of a religious community in Britain, recognizes that the enormous publicity which will focus on the Pope will have its good and bad points: 'Now that the Pope is coming to England, the first Pope ever to do so, he runs the risk of losing something by abandoning all that mystery, glamour and surrounding pomp. There could of course be compensating gains. First he will be and will seem to be less remote. He will be here among us and we will know that he has taken the trouble to come to be with us. Secondly, when he speaks, it will be to us in this island, not to the whole world.' But there will be deeper considerations affecting the national consciousness. No one with any sense of history can fail to be stirred by the significance of such a moment. No one can say how far there will be a further drawing together of the Church of Rome and the Anglican Communion as a consequence of his visit. Some will feel that recent progress in that direction has been too slow. Some, of whom I am certainly not one, may look on it as too rapid. Yet it is an irrefutable fact that progress has been and continues to be made and that the two Churches have never been so close as they are today since the Reformation.

There are those who doubt whether progress of this kind has been as rapid under the present Pope as it might have been under another Pontiff. Personally I see no reason to hold that view. He has never faltered in his passionate enthusiasm for the work of the Vatican Council, and the Vatican Council was an ecumenical event beyond all others. There will never be any going back to the previous disagreeable relationship. The Pope's extraordinary benevolence towards all mankind would make it psychologically impossible for him not to stretch out his hand to a Christian body that came halfway to meet him.

It must be admitted, however, that, brought up in Poland as he was, he has a limited awareness of Anglicanism. He is far closer physically and psychologically to the Orthodox Churches. At the

The British Prime Minister, Mrs Margaret Thatcher, was received at a private audience by Pope John Paul II in the Vatican on 24 November 1980.

time he became Pope he was bound to be more interested in unity with the Eastern rather than the Western Churches. But he is still relatively young with a great mental and physical vigour – now, it is to be hoped, fully restored. No limit should be set on the mutual understanding that may grow up between him and the Anglican leaders.

The Pope is known to be preparing most carefully for his visit. His preparation includes a profound study of the Church of England, especially the recent work of the Anglican/Roman Catholic International Commission's statements on the Eucharist, Authority and Ministry.

We can draw, surely, great encouragement from the immense success of the Queen's visit to John Paul II in autumn 1980, followed by one from the Prime Minister, Mrs Thatcher. There seems to have been an unmistakable *rapport* between the Pope and the Queen. Certainly they have much in common. Simplicity, dignity, integrity, readiness for total self-sacrifice and dedication to the family. It is to be hoped that, after the forthcoming visit of the Pope, the mutual understanding established between the Queen and himself will extend to all her subjects. The Labour politician, Robert Mellish, sums up the feelings of the Catholic community in Britain: 'His Holiness will be received with acclamation by all our people and we Catholics will take tremendous pride in his visit. He is truly one of the great men of our time and is living proof of what the Catholic Church is all about.'

Let the last words rest with Cardinal Hume: he describes John Paul II as a pastoral Pope, before all else. He does not, I am sure, only mean that Pope John Paul II wishes to proclaim his ideal to everyone on the planet, though he has expressed that purpose many times. Cardinal Hume sees him on the deepest level as a loving shepherd who cares for all his sheep, whether they be of his own fold or of some other, and whether they live up to his standards or, being human, fall below them.

Epilogue
Catholicism in Britain

THE STORY OF THE CATHOLICS in Britain since the break with Rome and the Catholic Church in the sixteenth century was for long years one of persecution, deprivation and suffering. They were deprived of their civil rights and banned by law from celebrating their faith. Their situation only began to improve in the nineteenth century with the growth of more liberal attitudes.

The break with Rome arose from political necessity rather than from spiritual beliefs. Henry VIII, who had been given the title 'Defender of the Faith' by Pope Leo X for his book written against the teachings of Martin Luther, wished to have his marriage to Catherine of Aragon declared null and void and to marry Anne Boleyn. The Papacy made it impossible theologically for Henry to divorce Catherine. In June 1534, the Act of Supremacy was placed upon the Statute book: 'Be it enacted by the authority of the present Parliament,' the Act begins, 'that the King our Sovereign Lord, his heirs and successors, Kings of this realm, shall be taken, accepted and reputed the only Supreme Head in earth of the Church of England called *Ecclesia Anglicana.*' All in positions of authority, both temporal and ecclesiastical, were required to take the oath of Supremacy.

The King further reinforced his position by the dissolution of the monasteries, carried out by Thomas Cromwell. These Catholic communities were broken up, their powers removed and their churches and abbeys destroyed. Although Henry met resistance from the great Catholic barons throughout the country, most Catholics were prepared to take the oath of Supremacy, while carrying on much as normal. But St John Fisher and St Thomas More refused to accept the oath. They were imprisoned in the Tower and executed in the summer of 1535 – among the first of many Catholics to suffer for their faith. Catholics were to be persecuted and denied their rights for the next three hundred years.

When Henry VIII died in 1547, he was succeeded by his young son, Edward VI, who was under the control of Protestant advisers. The Protestants advanced the establishment of their faith even further: the use of Latin in services was forbidden; images in churches were destroyed; the use of an English form of Common Prayer was made compulsory; and in 1552, 42 Articles of Religion and a new Prayer Book were published. There were pockets of Catholic resistance through the country such as the Western Rising and Ket's Rebellion in Norfolk in 1549. The risings were savagely put down. Hundreds of men died.

With Edward's death in 1553 came a temporary reversal of policy under Mary I. She was an ardent Catholic and married the Catholic King of Spain, Philip II. Her Parliament revoked the laws of Henry's Reformation and submitted to the Pope. Now it was the Protestants who were proclaimed heretics. Many fled to the continent and those who remained were persecuted, some being burned at the stake. Britain had returned to Catholicism. Mass and ancient rituals were restored, but the reversal was to be shortlived.

Elizabeth I succeeded Mary in 1558. One of the first acts of her Parliament of 1559 was to pass an Act of Supremacy. Clergy, judges, officials and university graduates had to take an oath acknowledging the Queen as Supreme Governor 'in all spiritual or ecclesiastical things as well as temporal'. An Act of Uniformity ruled that only the 1552 Book of Common Prayer was to be used in churches and there was a fine of twelve pence for non-attendance at church on Sundays.

Like her father, Elizabeth's main concern was political rather than religious: to ensure the unity of Church and State. She was determined to establish her popularity so firmly that no enemy, foreign or domestic, would secure any large measure of support. In England, the risings of the great peers of the realm were suppressed. She felt herself threatened by the claims of the Catholic Mary Stuart to the succession. Elizabeth had encouraged Mary's enemies and, as a result, Mary was forced to seek refuge in England in 1568 and became a focus of disaffection as long as she lived.

In February 1570, Pope Pius V had been persuaded that the Catholics in Britain had taken up arms for their faith and a papal bull pronounced Elizabeth a heretic and declared her deposed. It was a turning-point for the Catholics in Britain. Elizabeth responded by increasing the penalties for non-conformity. Anyone who accepted the ruling of the papal bull was to be declared a traitor. The laws against Catholics were enforced with increasing fervour.

Staunchly Catholic families who wished to continue their worship in secret constructed elaborate hiding-places for priests – in chimney-breasts, under the roofs, beneath staircases, in the thickness of the walls, between floors, even in disused sewers. These have become known as 'priest holes'.

During the 1570s many Catholics who refused to accept the suppression of the Catholic faith in Britain sent their sons abroad to be

A portrait of Henry VIII after Holbein

St Thomas More, his family
and descendents by
R. Lockley, 1593, after
Holbein

ordained. By the end of the sixteenth century, a growing number of these 'seminary' priests returned from the continent secretly. They were willing to face the imprisonment, torture and death that they could expect if they were captured. Execution was extremely barbarous. The condemned man was dragged through the streets to the gallows, hanged until half strangled, and then cut down, slashed open and his vital organs torn out.

Edmund Campion is the best known of these young priests. Campion had left Oxford for France in 1572. When he returned to England on his secret mission, he stated that his aim was to prove the truth of the Catholic faith and win England back to its observance. Campion became well known and popular throughout the country, but he was eventually captured in July 1581 and taken to the Tower. He was questioned by the Queen herself and argued that it was possible to be both a loyal Catholic and a loyal subject of the Queen. Although Elizabeth found him impressive, she could not accept his argument. Campion met his death on the gallows at Tyburn.

To British Catholics, it seemed that all hope of freedom died with the execution of Mary Queen of Scots in 1587. Most Catholics had hoped that she would succeed Elizabeth, although few had been prepared to become involved in the many plots to put her on the throne. Restrictions on Catholics were increased and persecution continued. But hopes were renewed when Mary's son, James I, succeeded to the throne of England on Elizabeth's death in 1603.

James I did take some steps on behalf of the Catholics. A large number of those in prison for their beliefs were released and he openly invited Catholics to his Court. But James was not prepared to go as far as expected. The Elizabethan penal laws against Catholics

Edmund Campion is led to his execution at Tyburn.

Robert
Winter

Christopher
wright

Iohn
wright

Thomas
Percy

Guido
Fawkes

Robert
Catesby

Thomas
Winter

Bates

Guy Fawkes and his fellow conspirators in a seventeenth-century engraving

were re-enacted because priests had begun to arrive openly in Britain. Catholics believed that James had acted in response to pressure from Parliament, and Robert Catesby headed a plot to blow up the Houses of Parliament. He enlisted the help of Thomas Winter, his brother-in-law, John Grant, two distant cousins, and a soldier-of-fortune, Guy Fawkes. They hid thirty-six casks of gunpowder under a pile of firewood in the cellars of the Houses of Parliament and Guy Fawkes was put in charge of them. Officials were fully aware of the plot and seized Guy Fawkes on the night of 4–5 November 1604. The conspirators either died fighting or were executed after questioning. No single event can ever have done more harm to the cause of British Catholics.

A number of prominent Catholics were sent to the Tower after the Gunpowder Plot and Catholic priests were hunted down, imprisoned and tortured. In 1606, more Acts were passed against Catholics: the sacrament had to be taken at least once a year with a fine for default; the oath of loyalty to James was made more difficult for Catholics to accept and the fine for not doing so was the loss of property. The Catholics' civil rights were whittled away. A reward of up to fifty pounds was paid to those who gave information which led to the arrest of anyone who said Mass.

The accession of Charles I in 1625 did not greatly affect the Catholic position. But Charles did marry a French Catholic, Henrietta Maria, who arrived in England with fifteen priests and a Bishop. The King's generally tolerant attitude to Catholicism met with criticism and some resistance in Court. When Charles II was restored to the throne after the years of the Protectorate under Cromwell, many Catholics had high hopes that his sympathies with Rome would lead him to repeal the Acts against them, but Parliament was not willing to do this. In the event, laws against non-conformists, whether Catholic or Protestant, were no less severe in order to maintain stability. It was still dangerous to attack the King openly, for fears of civil war lingered on.

The fantastic story of Titus Oates's 'Popish Plot' was set against this background of suspicion and fear which had overtaken the country. Titus Oates, who antagonized all he came into contact with, was admitted to the Society of Jesus but was later expelled for his outrageous behaviour. With the help of Israel Tonge, a friend of his father, Oates drew up a narrative describing an elaborate Jesuit plot for overthrowing Charles and establishing Catholic domination in England. The political enemies of the King seized this opportunity to undermine his position. Oates's accusations were published, although it was obvious that they were false, and Charles did not dare intervene. A time of fear and persecution followed for Catholics throughout the country. Houses were searched and looted, those accused by Oates were tried and Catholics were subjected to mob violence in the streets. Between 1678 and 1681, about two thousand people were imprisoned and seven priests and five laymen executed as traitors.

A satirical seventeenth-century engraving of the feared arrival of the Pope in London in 1679

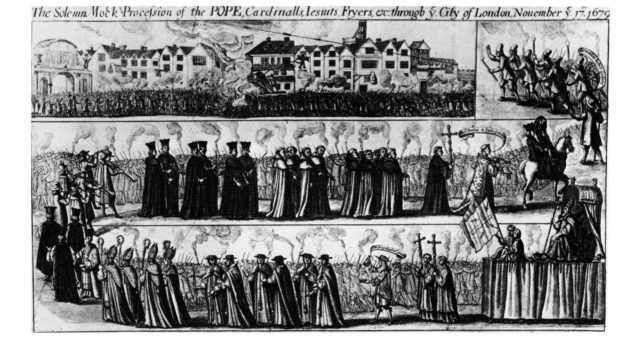

The Solemn Mock Procession of the POPE, Cardinalls, Iesuits, Fryers, &c: through ŷ City of London, Nouember ŷ. 17. 1679

The most sensational of the trials was that of Oliver Plunket, Archbishop of Armagh. He was charged in Ireland with involvement in the plot but there was found to be no evidence against him. So he was brought to England and imprisoned in Newgate. Plunket's trial was a mockery and he was executed on 1 July 1681.

The Popish Plot was the last organized persecution of Englishmen for religious reasons. James II became King in 1685 and, although he was a Catholic, he did not succeed in having the penal laws repealed; finally, his pro-Catholic sympathies caused the Whigs and Tories to unite in inviting Mary, James's daughter, and her husband William of Orange to take the throne and restore 'the liberties of the country'. As William and Mary entered London, James fled into exile. The Whig Ascendancy had come to stay. The King in exile drained away some of the most active elements among the Catholics.

During the first half of the eighteenth century the Catholics had never counted for less politically. The attempts of the Old Pretender in 1708 and 1715 and the Young Pretender, Bonnie Prince Charlie, in 1745 to regain power were total failures. But in the later years of the century things began to improve. With the birth of a less savage age, there was a widespread atmosphere of religious tolerance. In America the movement for independence which lead to open rebellion had highlighted the need for more soldiers in Britain. In 1777, it was decided that it would now be safe to use the Catholic Highlanders in Scotland as troops. There was also a Roman Catholic Relief Act in 1778 which met with little opposition. It was not a drastic move, but it was a start. It meant that Catholic priests were no longer subject to life imprisonment.

There was an immediate Protestant backlash. A Protestant association was formed, which in 1779 elected Lord George Gordon, a younger son of the Duke of Gordon, as its President. The so-called Gordon Riots followed. An enormous crowd collected at St George's Fields in London on 2 June 1780. The Archbishop of York, many other Bishops and a number of members of Parliament were assaulted. Eventually George III intervened by issuing a proclamation, but the troops were not called in until 8 June, when the mob was quickly scattered. By the end of the riots, two hundred and eighty-five people had been shot or died of their wounds and many more trampled to death. Twenty-one of the prisoners were executed. But the movement towards toleration and emancipation of Catholics could not be checked. For over two hundred years the saying and hearing of Mass had been prohibited under penalty of death. Now, under an Act passed in 1791, it was in effect permitted. The right to sit in Parliament and other liberties were still withheld.

The pressure for Catholic emancipation in the Parliamentary sense continued. The cause had suffered a setback at the time of the Irish Union of 1801. Pitt had promised the Catholic hierarchy in Ireland that emancipation would follow the Union. But the obduracy of George III compelled him to break this promise, whereupon he honourably resigned. The Catholic Emancipation Act of 1829 was the result of intense Irish agitation led by Daniel O'Connell, though many Englishmen had long espoused the reform. From now on, the influence of the Catholic Irish members of Parliament became a steadily increasing factor in English politics and with each reform bill they became more and more representative of their countrymen. They did not officially disappear from the Westminster scene until after the Anglo-Irish Treaty of 1921.

Throughout the nineteenth century Irish men and women had been flowing into the new centres of population in London, Bristol and, most of all, Liverpool. The appalling famine of 1846-51, which reduced the Irish population by millions through death and emigration, swelled the trickle of Irish to Britain into a mighty flood. Between 1841 and 1851, the Irish-born population in Britain doubled.

By the time that the famine in Ireland broke out, the Oxford Movement had been convulsing the Church of England for some years. The movement included many distinguished figures, of whom Newman and Manning, both destined to become Cardinals, were the most influential. A striking addition to the Catholic ranks from the high aristocracy was George Spencer, a forebear of the Princess of Wales. My own family at that time were strongly Protestant but one of my great-uncles left the Grenadier Guards to become a Catholic and then a Passionist monk. He and George Spencer worked among the poor in Dublin before my great-uncle's early death.

The year 1850 is famous for the official restoration of the Catholic hierarchy, that is to say their re-introduction into England. The manner in which this was proclaimed by Cardinal Wiseman, the first Catholic Archbishop of Westminster, led to frenzied protest. Lord John Russell, the Prime Minister, was well to the fore. The Cardinal, however, published an immensely effective appeal to the English people in which his charity towards his own flock and especially the poor was demonstrated for all to see.

The history of the Catholics in Britain from 1850 to 1982 has externally been little different from that of the general population. To write their story would be to attempt a history of Britain during that period with all its grandeurs and miseries, culminating in the sufferings undergone and the heroism exhibited during two world wars. Their spiritual life has remained their own, as has been the case with the other Christian communions and the Jews.

The Duke of Norfolk, the leader of the Catholic laity and head of the most famous Catholic family in England, sets the visit of Pope John Paul II in the context of the history of Catholicism in Britain since the break with Rome:

'Many of my friends sensibly see the papal visit as one of the concluding chapters of the healing of the cleavage of Christendom which sadly occurred in the sixteenth century.

'If the Emperor Charles V had not succeeded in delaying the meetings of the Council of Trent until 1545, and if his aunt, Queen Catherine of Aragon, had borne a living son to Henry VIII, the tired and corrupt medieval Church might have been rejuvenated without the secession of the Anglican Church and the German Protestants. The papal bull *Regnans in Excelsis* further widened the breach with England in 1570.

'But, in a typically British pragmatic and blurred way, the Stuarts had currents running against each other. James I regarded the Pope as *Princeps Episcoporum* and was very conscious of his mother's Catholicism. He saw nothing incongruous in burying Queen Elizabath I with Queen Mary in her grave.

'Charles I kept in contact with Rome through his Queen, Henrietta Maria, and in an attempt to heal the breach the possibility of making Archbishop Laud a Cardinal was discussed. Charles II too married a Catholic, Catherine of Braganza, and through her Almoner, Cardinal Howard, links with the Vatican were available. He ended his life by dying in the Catholic faith. James II's tolerant Catholic policy, however, ended the hope of an amicable English settlement and provoked the revolution of 1688, ushering in a century of Whig dominance.

'The nineteenth century started with rays of hope, such as the influx of Catholic French refugee priests, Catholic Emancipation in 1829, and the swelling of the Catholic population to a quarter of a million – a tenfold increase – by the arrival of the Irish fleeing from the terrible potato famine of 1846. But it proved to be a false dawn, with the untimely and, some thought, arrogant restoration of the Catholic hierarchy and the flamboyant Cardinal Wiseman issuing his "Out of the Flamian Gate" Proclamation. (How much easier would the work of the Anglican/Catholic ecumenists be if we were still ruled by Vicars Apostolic!!) And the Proclamation of the Syllabus of Errors and Papal Infallibility in 1870 by Pio Nono saw the flood ebb further away.

'But it turned with Lord Halifax and Cardinal Mercier meeting at Malines, and later the appointment of Cardinal Hinsley to Westminster during World War II, and his founding of the Sword of the Spirit, later called the Catholic Institute of International Relations. John XXIII's calling the Second Vatican Council and founding the

Secretariat of Christian Unity with the visit of Archbishop Fisher to Rome in 1960 set the scene for Archbishop Ramsay's reception in the Sistine Chapel by Pope Paul VI in 1966, when the Pope said, "By your coming you rebuild a bridge which for centuries has lain fallen between the Churches of Rome and Canterbury. Your steps bring you to a home which you can call your own."

'The canonization of the 40 Martyrs, instead of leading to contention, led Paul VI to say, "There will be no seeking to lessen the legitimate prestige and usage proper to the Anglican Church, when the Roman Catholic Church is able to embrace firmly her ever-beloved sister in the one authentic communion of the Family of Christ: a communion of origin, faith, priesthood and rule."

'The conclusions of the Anglican Roman Catholic International Commission, and the hopes of the Archbishop of Canterbury that

A drawing attributed to H. E. Doyle of Nicholas, Cardinal Wiseman (1802–1865), the first Cardinal at Westminster after the restoration of the Catholic hierarchy in 1850.

before the year 2,000 we would be recognizing the Anglican Holy Communion Service as Mass, lead my friends to believe ecumenism is bringing us closer every day. The first visit of a Pope to Britain will indeed be an important milestone.

'Sometimes I muse and wonder whether St Thomas More and Archbishop Cranmer are smiling in Heaven as the history of this twentieth century unfurls.'

My wife, Elizabeth Longford, an eminent historian, writing from our home in Chelsea, sees similarities between Thomas More and Pope John Paul II:

'The Pope's visit will stir many different thoughts in us, his British hosts. The philosophers among us will think especially of his acute philosophical mind. The poets will recognize his subtle poetic imagination. The workers will see in him a champion of their rights. But for a historian like myself his presence inevitably evokes certain deathless moments in English history.

'I live in Chelsea, near the vanished riverside home of St Thomas More, Henry VIII's Lord Chancellor, from which he was torn away and carried down-river to Traitors' Gate in 1534, next year to die for his faith on Tower Green. I remember, too, that other Thomas who was More's name saint. Archbishop Thomas Becket met his martyrdom at Canterbury in 1170.

'There are many things about Thomas More, my own favourite saint, which remind me of Pope John Paul II. They are both seen as men of exceptional learning, authors of books and poems. To both was given the power of submerging themselves in prayer for many hours at a time, More for three hours every morning before breakfast, though he was a layman not a churchman. Both had to face the challenges of autocracy, More from the King, Wojtyla from the Kremlin.

'Wit, jokes and cheerfulness are the hallmarks of each, the words "merry" and "merrily" being among More's favourites. He and his beloved daughter, Margaret Roper, would pray for one another, "that we may *merrily* meet in Heaven". Heaven was no towering Mount Olympus or Mount Sinai echoing to the thunders of a Jove or a Jaweh, but a place of love and merriment in Christ.

'The famous lines written about Thomas More by his friend Robert Whittinton in 1520 could apply equally to Karol Wojtyla: "More is a man of an angel's wit, and singular learning. He is a man of many excellent virtues. I know not his fellow. For where is the man in whom so goodly virtues of gentleness, lowliness and affability? And as time requireth, a man of marvellous mirth and pastimes, and sometimes of a sad gravity, as who say a man for all seasons."

218

John Henry, Cardinal Newman, 1801–1890. A painting by E. Dean, 1889. A convert to the Catholic faith from the Oxford Movement, Newman was received into the Catholic Church in 1845 and became a Cardinal in 1879.

'Another friend said of More that he was "never in a fume", nor can I imagine Pope John Paul "in a fume" either. They could both feel righteous indignation, but a "fume" never, for the word implies fussing, a neurotic state of mind incompatible with their notable spiritual composure and peace.

'With his loyalty to the Papacy, More would have rejoiced indeed if a sixteenth-century Pope of the calibre of John Paul could have descended on London. But Catholics, and indeed the great body of Christians in general, have had to wait until the twentieth century for this unique occasion. By standing on a green hillock in his garden, More could have seen London *en fête* and the papal barge perhaps being rowed up the Thames. Instead it was the royal barge of Henry VIII which would glide up the river to sweet music, bringing the King to visit his good friend, Sir Thomas. The King could not have enough of his friend's wit and learning, until Sir Thomas refused to take the new royal Oath of Supremacy. Then it was off with his head. More chose death rather than denial of papal supremacy.

'So the Reformation rolled forward, bringing with it new abuses as numerous as the ones it claimed to have swept away. In the old days, John Heywood, the Catholic poet, would often visit Thomas More's "enchanted spot" beside the Thames, with its "living tapestry" of trees and flowers. But his son Jasper, a Jesuit poet, narrowly escaped hanging and was banished for life. Many priests and laymen were tortured and executed more cruelly than was St Thomas More himself. It was only a year ago that English Catholics were assembling at Marble Arch (the former Tyburn) to remember the martyrdom and canonization of St Oliver Plunket. Protestants had their martyrs too.

'At length the physical persecutions in England came to an end with the birth of a more tolerant age. Later still, exactly halfway through the last century, in 1850, Pope Pius IX boldly and spectacularly restored the English hierarchy. Bishop Nicholas Wiseman became, at forty-eight, the first English Cardinal for many hundreds of years. No doubt a few outraged extremists considered he was far from being a "wise man"; in fact a very foolish man to publicize the Church and so provoke renewed opposition. A year afterwards, at the wildly popular Crystal Palace Exhibition, a winged statue of St Michael striking down Satan was thought by some to be Queen Victoria expelling the Pope. The Queen herself, however, deplored any vilification of her Catholic subjects and their new Bishops. She found the "violent" attacks on their religion personally "painful". Her son, the Prince of Wales, was allowed to visit His Holiness nine years later, and as King Edward VII he went again to the Vatican in 1903. And as everyone knows, Pope John XXIII received Queen Elizabeth the Queen Mother and Princess Margaret in 1959, while twenty-one years later Queen Elizabeth II and Prince Philip were received by Pope John Paul II.'

For Catholics in Britain, life has changed remarkably in recent years. In the past they have predominantly belonged to the poorer sections of the community, but their standard of living this century has improved a good deal more than the average. Certainly they have become much more prominent in the professions and business, though more in the former than the latter. When I was an undergraduate at Oxford fifty-odd years ago, I was only aware of the

OPPOSITE The interior of Westminster Cathedral during the Maundy Thursday Mass.

220

presence of two Catholic dons. Now I am told there are at least one hundred. We have seen a Catholic editor of *The Times*, a Catholic Director-General of the BBC and, still more strikingly perhaps, a Catholic editor of the radical *New Statesman*. The way has now been made open by legislation for a Catholic to become Lord Chancellor. No one supposes that, if a Catholic were chosen as Prime Minister, he or she would be debarred by faith. That would have been incredible not so many years ago. In recent years, Labour Cabinets have included such Catholics as Mr Robert Mellish, Mrs Shirley Williams and myself: on the Conservative side, Mr Norman St John Stevas and Lord Windlesham. Windlesham and myself have been Leaders of the House of Lords. Norman St John Stevas has been Leader of the House of Commons, and Robert Mellish Chief Whip in a Labour Government.

The forty years since my own conversion to Catholicism can be neatly divided into two: pre-Council and post-Council. Within our own Church the far-reaching changes in the liturgy which came out of the Council have been accepted loyally by all, and enthusiastically by the great majority, although mournfully by a limited number for whom the Church is their life. I am sure that my wife, a convert like myself, speaks for most Catholics today when she says that the ritual participation of the congregation in the liturgy has been an expanding inspiration in recent years. Another vitally important outcome of the Council was of course the enormous contribution it made towards the ecumenical movement, the coming together of the Churches. With this subject uppermost in our minds on this momentous occasion, this time I leave the last words to my wife: 'Today the unity of Christendom is the hope of the world. The visit of Pope John Paul II to this "offshore island" will surely bring that day nearer. "Offshore" the United Kingdom may be. But history tells us, through the stories of her saints, that this kingdom has never lost touch with the universal church, nor failed to transcend her own narrow seas. How the two great English Thomases, Becket and More, would have gloried in this year's historic event, when the tide flowed again both ways.'

Index